Isaa
for Every Day

OTHER BOOKS IN THE SERIES

Isaac Hecker
for Every Day

*Daily Thoughts from the
Founder of the Paulists*

Edited by
Ronald A. Franco, CSP

Paulist Press
New York/Mahwah, NJ

Cover design by Sharyn Banks
Book design by Lynn Else

Library of Congress Cataloging-in-Publication Data

Hecker, Isaac Thomas, 1819–1888.
    Isaac Hecker for every day : daily thoughts from the founder
of the Paulists / edited by Ronald A. Franco.
        p. cm.
    Includes bibliographical references (p.   ).
    ISBN 978-0-8091-4625-3 (alk. paper)
    1. Devotional calendars—Catholic Church. 2. Catholic
Church—Prayers and devotions. 3. Hecker, Isaac Thomas,
1819–1888—Meditations. I. Franco, Ronald A. II. Title.
    BX2170.C56H43 2009
    242'.2—dc22
                                                    2009016209

Published by Paulist Press
997 Macarthur Boulevard
Mahwah, New Jersey 07430

www.paulistpress.com

Printed and bound in the United States of America

Contents

Servant of God, Isaac Thomas Hecker, CSP
Founder of the Paulist Fathers

General Introduction

This short book seeks to share the thinking and spirituality of the Servant of God Isaac Thomas Hecker, founder of the Missionary Society of Saint Paul the Apostle (the Paulist Fathers), on a daily basis in the context of the calendar year.

Isaac Hecker was born into a German American family in New York City on December 18, 1819. As his older brothers' flour business became increasingly prosperous, Isaac shared their interest in political and social reform but increasingly focused more on a personal religious and spiritual search. Although his mother was a devout Methodist, Hecker himself examined the principal Protestant churches in the United States, as well as Unitarianism and Mormonism, and found himself a temporary haven among the New England transcendentalists, even living for several months in 1843 at the utopian communities of Brook Farm and Fruitlands. Yet, while benefiting from that environment, which encouraged him to value and explore his inner life, Hecker consistently maintained a certain intellectual independence from the beliefs of the Transcendentalists, enabling his exploration of his soul to lead to conclusions quite different from what the Transcendentalists believed. He came to understand his inner spiritual experience in terms of the action of the Holy Spirit and felt himself drawn more and more to the visible, structured, institutional Church. His early identification of Divine Providence with the Indwelling Holy Spirit made theological sense of the continuity between nature and grace, which he felt from his own experience, thus easing his way into the Church and laying the groundwork for his mature thought about the relationship between Church and society and the evangelization of the latter by the former. This commitment to the Church as the institutional expression of the presence and providential action of the Holy Spirit sustained him throughout his life, despite the difficulties he would experience.

Spurred by the conversion of his friend and intellectual mentor Orestes Brownson (1803–76), Isaac Hecker was received into the Roman Catholic Church by Bishop John McCloskey (later the first American cardinal) at Old Saint Patrick's Cathedral in New York, on August 1, 1844. His older brother George soon followed Isaac into the Church, and the two were confirmed together on May 18, 1845. Hecker's immediate practical task as a new Catholic was to find his vocation within the Church. Apparently, he had already committed himself to a celibate life, and now considered becoming a priest. In 1845, he met two other new Catholics, who were planning to travel to Europe to enter the Redemptorist order. Hecker decided to join them. After a year's novitiate in Belgium and a further three years at the Redemptorist house of studies in the Netherlands, he was sent to England to finish his formation and, on October 23, 1849, he was ordained a priest. Academically, it had been a difficult experience, but Hecker found it spiritually enriching, and he emerged well grounded in his new faith.

In 1851, he was sent back to the United States to participate in the preaching of parish missions. The group's first parish mission in New York was the first-ever English-language mission in the United States. Hecker reported that 6,000 persons went to confession and communion, while sobbing filled the church during the renewal of baptismal vows. It was while working on the missions that Hecker first addressed his non-Catholic countrymen in print, producing two books, *Questions of the Soul* (1855) and *Aspirations of Nature* (1857). They immediately established Hecker as one of the leading spokesmen for Roman Catholicism in the United States.

In 1857, Hecker with four other American-born, formerly Protestant Redemptorists—Augustine Hewit, George Deshon, Francis Baker, and Clarence Walworth—appealed directly to the Redemptorist authorities in Rome for an English-speaking American house primarily focused on missionary work, an idea that had originated with the previous provincial superior, but which his successor seemed to have reservations about. Hecker traveled to Rome, his expenses paid for by his brother George and armed with supportive letters from leading U.S. bishops. His Redemptorist superiors summarily expelled him from the community. Hecker responded with surprising serenity. He appealed his case to the Congregation of Propaganda, which, as the curial body in charge of the Church in mission territories, then had jurisdiction over the U.S. Church. Meanwhile, his four colleagues back home petitioned to be dispensed from their Redemptorist vows. This was granted on March 6, 1858, in a decree which joined Hecker's case to that of the other four and directed them to continue their work under the direction and jurisdiction of the local bishops.

Back in New York, on July 7, 1858, Hecker and three of his colleagues—Hewit, Deshon, and

Baker—formed what became the Missionary Society of Saint Paul the Apostle, commonly known as the Paulist Fathers. The four took charge of a new parish on the West Side of Manhattan and began their mission as a community. Hecker's priorities during this period concentrated primarily on pastoral and missionary work. During the Civil War, with parish missions necessarily suspended, Hecker continued to lecture widely. In 1865, he founded a monthly magazine, *The Catholic World*, the effective beginning of the Paulist Press; and, in 1866, he addressed the Second Plenary Council of Baltimore on "The Future Triumph of the Church." In 1869–70, Hecker returned to Rome for the First Vatican Council, a pivotal event in the development of his understanding of the relationship between external Church authority and the internal action of the Holy Spirit.

In the 1870s, as his health began to decline, Hecker's activity (although not his writing) diminished. A trip to Europe, Egypt, and the Holy Land did nothing to restore his health, but it did have a profound spiritual effect and also significantly broadened his interest beyond the United States. On Saturday, December 22, 1888, Isaac Hecker died at the Paulist parish in New York. In 1959, his body was transferred to the monumental sarcophagus in the parish church, the construction of which he had taken such a great interest in. In 2006, the Paulist Fathers General Assembly resolved to promote the cause of Isaac Hecker's canonization as a saint. His cause was formally opened by the Archbishop of New York, Edward Cardinal Egan, at Saint Paul the Apostle Church, on January 27, 2008.

As a young man, Hecker had allowed himself to be guided by the Holy Spirit, whose presence and action he discerned in God's providential care for him, and from whom he received the grace to recognize and follow in the Roman Catholic Church. His enthusiastic embrace of the Church led him to a vocation as a priest and religious, and formed him, in spite of difficulties and challenges, into an active and thoroughly committed missionary for the Church in the United States. As founder of the Paulist Fathers, he concentrated on the Church's perennially essential mission of evangelization, both within the Church and outward to the world—planting his vision in the solid soil of the first American men's religious community and their growing parish in New York. Finally, in the last period of his life, immersed in his own dark night of the soul, he surrendered himself—and all his activities—to the call to conform his life to the mystery of Christ's cross—*completing*, in the words of his patron St.

Paul, *what is lacking in Christ's afflictions for the sake of his body, that is, the church* (Col 1:24).

Selections for these reflections have been taken directly from Hecker's books, articles, and letters, and occasionally from conversations recorded by his contemporaries. There has been minimum editing of spelling and punctuation, neither of which had yet been standardized at the time. The original spelling and punctuation also help retain Hecker's distinctive language and style, especially that in his diary.

January

Hecker's Experience of God Directing His Life and Leading Him toward His Vocation and Mission

Both at the time and later looking back on the course of his life, Servant of God Isaac Thomas Hecker was serenely conscious of God's providence and confident that there was a mission for him in God's providential plan. We begin our year-long journey with Hecker with some of his own reflections on key moments of his life—from his spiritually sensitized youth; to his self-conscious religious quest; to his conversion to Roman Catholicism and his enthusiastic embrace of his new faith; to his life as a Redemptorist seminarian and priest, a missionary in his own homeland,

and, finally, the founder of the Paulist Fathers, the first American religious community of men.

The texts for this month are all taken from the book *The Paulist Vocation*.

1

Once in my childhood I was given over for death, having been taken down with the smallpox. My mother came to my bedside and told me that I was going to die. I answered her: "No, mother, I shall not die now; God has a work for me to do in the world, and I shall live to do it." (From statements made by Father Hecker towards the end of his life; *PV*, 3)

2

Born of Protestant parents and in the midst of a Protestant community, no positive religious instructions were imparted to me in my youth, and my religious belief, therefore, was left for me to decide...at some future period and according to my own choice. At the early age of twelve years my mind began to seek after the truth, and my heart was moved with the desire of doing to others. (Document submitted by Father Hecker to his director and others, Rome, 1858; *PV*, 49)

3

Often in my boyhood, when lying at night on the shavings before the oven in the bake house, I would start up, roused in spite of myself, by some great thought....What does God desire from me? How shall I attain unto Him? What is it He has sent me into the world to do? These were the ceaseless questions of my heart, that rested, meanwhile, in an unshaken confidence that time would bring the answer. (From statements made by Father Hecker towards the end of his life; *PV*, 3)

4

Several years of study and effort in the way of political reform made it evident that the evils of society were not so much political as social.... Hence a social reform was called for, and this led me into the examination of the social evils of the present state of society. The many miseries and the great wretchedness that exist in modern society sprung, in my opinion, from the want of the practical application of the moral principles of Christianity to the social relations between men. (Document submitted by Father Hecker to his director and others, Rome, 1858; *PV*, 51)

5

Why should not those who profess Christianity imitate Christ in devoting themselves entirely to the spreading of the truth, the relief of the poor, and the elevation of the lower classes? Such like thoughts occupied my mind, and since a social reform was needed, it was my duty to begin with myself, and this led me to treat those in my employ with greater kindness, and to make important changes in my way of living. (Document submitted by Father Hecker to his director and others, Rome, 1858; *PV*, 51)

6

It became clear to me that the evils of society were not so much social as personal, and it was not by a social reform they would be remedied, but by a personal one. This turned my attention to religion which has for its aim the conversion and reformation of the soul. (Document submitted by Father Hecker to his director and others, Rome, 1858; *PV*, 52)

7

The question then presented itself in this shape: either the truth is to be found in the Catholic Church, the place where it is supposed among Protestants the least to exist, or God will yet reveal it, for it is not reasonable to suppose that He would implant in the soul such an ardent thirst for truth and not reveal it. (Document submitted by Father Hecker to his director and others, Rome, 1858; *PV*, 52)

8

God at length conquered, and led me to make this entire renunciation, and to be willing to be poor, despised, and alone in the world. It was then that the Catholic Church burst upon my vision as the object to which all my efforts had been unintentionally directed. It was not a change, but a sudden realization of all that had hitherto obscurely captivated my mind, and secretly attracted my heart. (Document submitted by Father Hecker to his director and others, Rome, 1858; *PV*, 53)

9

On my reception into the Church no abjuration was exacted, since my assent was never given to any sect or form of error; and the only desire that occupied me was to devote myself wholly to God and His service. (Document submitted by Father Hecker to his director and others, Rome, 1858; *PV*, 53)

10

My noviciate was one of sore trials, for the master of novices seemed not to understand me, and the manifestation of my interior to him was a source of the greatest pain. After about nine or ten months he appeared to recognize the hand of God in my direction in a special manner, conceived a great esteem, and placed an unusual confidence in me, and allowed me, without asking it, though greatly desired, daily communion. (Document submitted by Father Hecker to his director and others, Rome, 1858; *PV*, 53–54)

11

A doubt of my religious vocation never entered my mind nor was it once suggested by my novice master. Some fears, however, at not being able to pursue my studies in that state arose in my mind, but he bade me banish them, and my vows were made at the end of the year. (Document submitted by Father Hecker to his director and others, Rome, 1858; *PV*, 54)

12

It seemed to me in looking back on my career before becoming a Catholic, that Divine Providence had led me as it were by the hand, through the different ways of error, and made me personally acquainted with the different classes of person (and their wants) of which the people of the United States is composed, in order that having made known to me the truth He might employ me the better to point out to them the way to His Church. That, therefore, my vocation was to labor for the conversion of my non-Catholic fellow countrymen. (Document submitted by Father Hecker to his director and others, Rome, 1858; *PV*, 55)

13

This work at first was, it seemed to me, to be accomplished by means of acquired science, but now it had been made plain that God would have it done principally by the aid of His grace; and if left to study at such moments when my mind was free, it would not take a long time for me to acquire sufficient knowledge to be ordained a priest. (Document submitted by Father Hecker to his director and others, Rome, 1858; *PV*, 55–56)

14

During this period my abasement and helplessness continued and were increased, and so much so that it baffles all my powers of expression. It seemed as though the slightest action of my mind or body depended altogether and directly on

God....And it also seemed to me that God required of me to accept this abject condition for my whole life, and after some struggle this act of acceptance was made. (Document submitted by Father Hecker to his director and others, Rome, 1858; *PV*, 56)

15

Immediately after my ordination my superiors employed me in the work of missions. The duties of the sacred ministry appeared to me most natural, the hearing of confessions and the direction of souls was as though it had been a thing practiced from my childhood, and was a source of great consolation. (Document submitted by Father Hecker to his director and others, Rome, 1858; *PV*, 56)

16

Such strong and deep impulses, and so vast in their reach, took possession of my soul on my return to the United States in regard to the conversion of the American people that on manifesting my interior to one of the most spiritually enlightened and experienced fathers of the [Redemptorist] Congregation on the subject (Father Rumpler) to obtain his direction, he bade me "not to resist these interior movements—they come from God—and that He would yet employ me in accordance with them." (Document submitted by Father Hecker to his director and others, Rome, 1858; *PV*, 57)

17

One day alone in my cell the thought suddenly struck me how great were my privileges and my joy since becoming a Catholic, and how great were my troubles and agony of soul before this event....This thought, and with it the hope of inducing young men to enter into religious orders, produced in a few months from my pen a book entitled *Questions of the Soul*. The main features of this book are...showing that the sacraments of the Catholic Church satisfy fully all the wants of the heart, and that the desire of leading a life of Christian perfection can only be realized in the religious orders of the Catholic Church. (Document submitted by Father Hecker to his director and others, Rome, 1858; *PV*, 58)

18

But the head was left yet to be converted. This thought led me to write a second book called *Aspirations of Nature*, which has for its aim to show that the truths of the Catholic faith answer completely to the demands of reason. My purpose in these two books was to explain the Catholic religion in such a manner as to reach and attract the minds of the non-Catholics of the American people. These books were regarded in my own secret thoughts as the test whether God had really given me the grace and vocation to labor in a special manner for the conversion of these people. (Document submitted by Father Hecker to his director and others, Rome, 1858; *PV*, 58)

19

If God has called me to such a work, His Providence has in a singular way, since my arrival at Rome, opened the door for me to undertake it. The object of my coming to Rome was to induce the [Redemptorist] General to sustain and favor the extension of our missionary labors in the United States. It was undertaken altogether in the good of the order, the general interests of religion, and in undoubted good faith. (Document submitted by Father Hecker to his director and others, Rome, 1858; *PV*, 61)

20

Under false impressions of my purpose, my expulsion from the Congregation was decreed three days after my arrival. This was about three months ago, and was the source of the deepest affliction to me, and up to within a short time my great desire was to re-enter the Congregation. At present it seems to me that these things were permitted by Divine Providence in order to place me in the position to undertake that mission which has never ceased to occupy my thoughts. (Document submitted by Father Hecker to his director and others, Rome, 1858; *PV*, 61)

21

So far, no step that has been taken on our part need be regretted; if it were to be done over again it would have my consent; the blow given to me I have endeavored to receive with humility in view of God; it has not produced any trouble in my soul, nor made me waver in the slightest degree in my confidence in God or in my duty towards Him. Let us not be impatient; God is with us, and will lead us if we confide in him. (From a letter to his brother George V. Hecker, Rome, September 2, 1857; *PV*, 31)

22

If God wishes to make use of us as instruments in such a design, and I can be assured of this on *competent authority*, with His grace, whatever it may cost, I will not shrink from it. (From a letter to the American Fathers, Rome, September 1857; *PV*, 35)

23

You will remember, and, I hope, before this reaches you, have answered my proposition in my last note, whether you would be willing to form an independent band of missionaries, to be devoted to the great wants of the country? I have considered and reconsidered, and prayed and prayed, and in spite of my fears, this seems to be the direction [to] which Divine Providence calls us. (From a letter to the American Fathers, Rome, September 1857; *PV*, 36–37)

Considering our past training and many other advantages which we possess, I cannot but believe that God will use us, providing we remain faithful to Him, united together as one man, and ready to make any sacrifices, for some such a holy enterprise; and my daily prayer is that the Holy Father may receive a special grace and inspiration to welcome and bless such a proposition. (From a letter to the American Fathers, Rome, December 9, 1857; *PV*, 42)

25

The Conversion of Saint Paul

God has bestowed on me great success, for all who know me here are my warm friends, and those acquainted with my affairs promise me great success. All depends on God; in the meantime I keep myself in my humility....God evidently has been in all these events, and...my stay here has not been useless. Indeed, I know that I am another man from what I was on coming here. No worse, I trust in God, but much better, greater zeal, heroism, submission to God. Indeed this has laid in me the foundations of something much greater than the world imagines—that of becoming a saint; for I am sure my present opportunities on that score are abundant, and, thank God, His grace is more abundant.

(From a letter to his brother George V. Hecker, Rome, December 18, 1857; *PV*, 43–44)

26
Saints Timothy and Titus, Companions of Saint Paul

No one is more aware of what such an enterprise demands and will cost, as sketched out, than I am, and if it be not clearly the will of God in my regard I will be glad to escape it. But should it prove to be His will, then I am ready to stand alone, pay the costs, and suffer any treatment. (From a letter to his brother George V. Hecker, Rome, January 2, 1858; *PV*, 47)

27

I must confess to you frankly that thoughts of this kind do occupy my mind and day by day they appear to come more clearly from heaven. I cannot refuse to entertain them without resisting what appears to me the inspirations of God. You know that these are not new opinions hastily adopted. From the beginning of my Catholic life there seemed always before me, but not distinctly, some such work, and it is indicated both in *Questions of the Soul* and the *Aspirations of Nature* and I cannot resist the thought that my present peculiar position is, or may be, providential to further some such undertaking. (From a letter to the American Fathers, Rome, January 1, 1858; *PV*, 47–48)

28

You may imagine that these views which I have expressed may only be a ruse of the devil to thwart our common cause and future prospects. If it be he, I shall head him off, because all that regards my personal vocation I shall submit to wise and holy men, and obey what they tell me. (From a letter to the American Fathers, Rome, January 1, 1858; *PV*, 48)

29

We are left in entire liberty to act in the future as God and our intelligence shall point the way. Let us be thankful to God, humble towards each other and everyone else, and more than ever in earnest to do the work God demands at our hands. (From a letter to the American Fathers, Rome, March 11, 1858; *PV*, 66)

30

Our aim is to lead a strict religious life in community, starting with the voluntary principle; leaving the question of vows to further experience, counsel, and indications of Divine Providence. Our principal work is the missions, such as we have hitherto given, but we are not excluded from other apostolic labors as the wants of the Church may demand or develop....One thing I may say, and I trust without boasting, we are of one mind and heart, resolved to labor and die for Jesus Christ, for the good of His Holy Church, for the advancement of the Catholic faith. (From a letter to a friend, New York, 1858; *PV*, 81)

31

We have the encouragement of a number of bishops, and also, we trust, the prayers, sympathy, and assistance of the faithful. We shall have to face obstacles, opposition from friends and foes; but if we are the right kind of men and have the virtues which such a position as ours demands, our trials will only strengthen us and make us the better Christians. (From a letter to a friend, New York, 1858; *PV*, 81)

February

Hecker's Search for God

From January 1842 to July 1845, as his spiritual search intensified—culminating in his 1844 conversion to Roman Catholicism and his decision to join the Redemptorists the following year—Hecker kept a remarkable diary. We continue our day-by-day exploration of Hecker's intensely personal experience of being drawn by God's grace, accompanying him, through the pages of his diary, during those uniquely transforming years. Many of the earlier entries reflect his association with the New England transcendentalists and his sojourn in 1843 at the utopian communities of Brook Farm and Fruitlands, while the later entries recount his final journey into the Church and his first steps to discern his vocation within it.

The texts for this month are all taken directly from Hecker's now-published diary.

1

Oh almighty Gracious Father who gavest me life wilt thou bless and graciously lead me in the study I am about to undertake. Give me always bounteously of thy Spirit and direct me in the true path in which I ought to go that I may inherit eternal life....Oh may I become an instrument of thine in doing much good. Lord I am weak nothing nothing oh Lord and in thy hands commit I my spirit. Do with me oh Lord as seemth good in thy sights. I feel willing to leave all for thee nay Lord lead me to thy Holy Church which I now am seeking for by the aid I hope of thy Holy Spirit. Wilt thou lead me in the road by which I may come into Thy fold even as it seemth good to thee. Amen. (Prayer written on the opening leaves of vol. 1 of Hecker's diary; *Diary*, 93)

2

Yesterday, as I was praying the thought flashed across my mind. Where is God? Is he not here? Why prayest thou as if He is at a great distance from thee. Where canst thou place him. Think of it. Where canst thou place him. What locality? Is he not here in thy midst. Is his presence not nearest thee. Oh think of it. God is here. His presence is allways, universal and nearest. Am I impious to say that the language used in scripture for Christ's expresses the thoughts of my soul. Oh could we but understand that the Kingdom of heaven is always *at hand* to the discerner. (April 20, 1843; *Diary*, 96)

3

It is only through Christ we can see the Love and Goodness & wisdom of God. He is to us what the microscope is to the Astronomer, with this difference. He exalts purifies us that our subject becomes the power to see. The microscope is a medium through which the boundaries of our vision are enlarged but is only passive. Christ is an active Mediator who begets us if we will and gives us power to see by becoming one with him. (April 28, 1843; *Diary*, 99)

4

Oh Lord. Lord forgive me my sins and save me from all errors and lead me in the path that thou wouldst have me to go. Is there no one who I can go to that may open my eyes that I may see. Oh Lord direct me. And if thou directest me now give me faith in thy means. I am, Oh Father, one of thy children: thou knowest all that I do. My heart is open to thy inspection. Do not let me suffer for thou art tender compassionate and full of love. Let me see: open thou my eyes, and grant that I may hear thy voice more distinctly. (June 19, 1843; *Diary*, 109–10)

5

Are we Christians if we act not in the spirit which Christ acted. Shall we say what we shall do? Follow the Spirit of Christ which is in you "unless ye are reprobates ye have it in you" wherever however and withsoever it lead you. Be ye faithfull as I am said Jesus. Love one another as I have Loved you. Take up your cross and follow him. Leave all if the Spirit leades you to leave all. Do whatever it leades you to do. There will not be any lack of action. Let him be all in all. (June 26, 1843; *Diary*, 112)

6

Oh heavenly Father wilt thou give me grace and strength to keep getting better to over come all temptations that may beset my path. Oh Lord awaken me more to the divine capacities thou hast endowed Man with and willt thou make my sight clearer and my hearing delicater that I may see more and more of thy law and hear more and more of thy divine voice of love. (August 9, 1843; *Diary*, 130)

7

Oh may I become more obedient meek Humble like Jesus Christ my master Lord and saving Redeemer to whom and to thee and to the holy spirit my soul is indebted wholly without measure. Oh make my heart more devout; inspire my soul; raise my thoughts and may thy spirit dwell in me in fullness to over flowing. Lord help me to over come all selfwill [and] to crucify self so that there may be nothing of the old Man left and that I may be a new Man born begotten in the Lord Jesus Christ who in heaven on the right hand of God giving help to all those who ask in sincerity and truth. (August 9, 1843; *Diary*, 130–31)

8

Now oh Lord I ask in Jesus's name give unto me more and more of thy loving spirit. Fill my whole being that there may not remain any thing but thy loving kindness. My soul is bowed down before thee oh Lord. Bless and bestow unto me thy gift heavenly Father. Amen. (August 9, 1843; *Diary*, 131)

9

We are called at times to rely on Providence to be according to the world and its wisdom imprudent and reckless. So I am willing to be thought. Each one of us has an individual character to act out to realize *under the inspiration of God* and this is the highest the noblest we can do. We are forms differing from one another and if we are acting with the inspiration of the Highest we are doing all that we can do; more the angels do not. (September 9, 1843; *Diary*, 138)

10

Did all our effort flow into realizing the teachings of the Spirit, we should do much more good and be greater in the sight of God than we are now by so much speaking and writing. But let us be watchfull that the pride of good works does not take place of that of speaking and writing. (September 24, 1843; *Diary*, 140)

11

It is the realization of the inspiration of God in and through us which is the Dial of our life. All other knowledge is but dross and as Paul says "dung." The knowledge of God is all and every thing; it is the knowledge of the mystery and secret of all things. He that knoweth God knoweth all things. Oh let us strive after a closer acquaintance with him a more intimate intercourse a more perfect union a greater confidence and trust in His almighty loving-kindness. (September 24, 1843; *Diary*, 141)

12

The Lord has been good unto me and my heart is filled with his warm love. Blessed be thou oh God for thou hast given me a taste of thy sweetness....Thou hast put into my heart gratitude and thankfullness and an over flowing heart of praise. I would stand still and shout and bless God. It is God in us that believes in God. Without the light of God we should be in total darkness and he is the only source of light. (September 24, 1843; *Diary*, 141)

13

Are we once born of the spirit we shall be led by it in all reforms to do and to abstain from all things which are an hindrance an obstruction to the full and complete harmonious life of the spirit in us. And he who cannot see the enemys of the spirit which he indulges proves only his one blindness consequent on his faithlessness for there is no virtue which the spirit does not teach if we would hear its whispering voice in our hearts. (November 1, 1843; *Diary*, 145)

14

The miser is an outward example of what the Christian should cheerfully do from the spirit of God living within. What does not the miser do for his God Mammon? Should not the Christian be willing to do for his God, Love and Wisdom. Ah would only Christians take the example of the miser in his abstinence in sacrificing all things to the one object. Do for the establishment of Christ's kingdom upon Earth what he does for money. (November 1, 1843; *Diary*, 145)

15

Oh Lord wilt thou guide me and lead me no matter in what pain or distress I may have to pass through to the true path which thou wouldst have me to go in. Oh I thank thee for all that thou hast in any way inflicted me. It has been to me the greatest blessing I could have received. And oh Lord chasten me more for I need it. How shall I live that I may be the best I can be under my conditions? And if these conditions in which I am placed are not the best where shall I go or how shall I change them. Teach me oh Lord and hear my humble prayer. (November 4, 1843; *Diary*, 146)

16

It is a great blindness of Men that they do not see Christ in the midst of us now leading, teaching, and exhorting us how we should live, and what we shall do....We are what we are through the medium of Christ the Redeemer. Take away the existence of Christ [and] what would we have been now? Is he not so far as we are better than we would have been without him all in all? (November 4, 1843; *Diary*, 146)

17

How does Jesus commune with humanity through the Church?...He promised to be with his disciples even unto the end of the world. To send them the Comforter which should lead them into all truth. That he would intercede for us to the Father etc. The Church holds that its Sacraments and forms are the visible means of communing with the invisible. The answer of the Church is that there is an invisible grace imparted to the worthy receiver through the visible forms of the Church; this is her answer. Is it true that such a grace is imparted? If it is it will be shown by its fruits. (November 15, 1843; *Diary*, 148)

18

Oh Lord keep me from all worldly ambition; keep my eye singly upon Thee. Oh heavenly parent kind father give me strength to persevere in goodness selfdenial and all holy aspirations. Oh Lord I am weak wavering; wilt thou give me power and firmness. Help me oh Lord to control and keep my appetites in subjection. Make me willing to be nothing for Thee. Burn out of me all earthly dross by whatever afflictions are necessary in thy sight. If I am better I know I shall see the work thou woulds have me to do. (November 17, 1843; *Diary*, 148)

19

When I cast my eyes back it seems to me that I have made some progress that I have grown somewhat better than I was. Thoughts feelings & passions which were active in my bosom whose character were not to be well spoken of in truth have disappeared and given place I hope to a better state of mind. Although my present state of mind is far from what I would have it to be, it is where I never anticipated it would be. (December 14, 1843; *Diary*, 153)

20

And now Oh God if thou helpest not I shall be worse than before. Heavenly Father as the flower depends upon the light and warmth of the sun for its growth and beauty much more do I depend upon Thee for life and progress. Oh Lord from the depths of my heart I would implore Thee to give me strength to aid me in all good intentions. Oh my heart overflows with its fullness of gratitude for what Thou hast done for me. And I know Thou willt not shorten thy hand or lessen Thy love. Therefore if I will come in an humble contrite and child like disposition Thou willt give me more of thy Grace and Truth. (December 14, 1843; *Diary*, 153)

21

Lord let me see more of Thee. Open thou more of my vision. Give me a purer heart. Let me rest wholly upon thee. Make me feel this. Oh Lord I feel this but the struggle of my soul to see thee more completely and help Thou in its attempts. Thy beauty Thy loveliness oh God is beyond our finite vision far above our expression and Lord all I can utter is help my weakness. (December 14, 1843; *Diary*, 153–54)

22
Feast of the Chair of Saint Peter

Catholicism is humanity becoming in an organized order....The different Societies institutions and unions in the Catholic Church are the naturel developement of the needs of Men under the influence of the Christian dispensation and so long as Men remain under that dispensation they will respond to their pressing wants. (January 1844; *Diary*, 157)

23

The Lord be merciful to me and forgive all my offences. As I am finite I sin. Increases my finiteness that I might embrace more of Thee oh Lord. Infuse in my soul more and more of thy love. Oh may my Soul's capacities for thee be enlarged. Tho I am nothing yet will I be contented and satisfied if Thou willt fill my small vessel with thy Glory. If I would be greater it is that I might containe more of thy Love and Light. It is us oh Lord I know that place hindrences in our Souls to Thee. Lead me oh to remove them from thy Sight. Heavenly Father teach and counsel me as a child. May all presumption willfulness and worldly ambition be purged out of me with Thy pure love. (February 19, 1844; *Diary*, 160–61)

24

I feel the presence of God where ever I am. I would kneel and praise God in all places. In His presence I walk and feel His breath encompass me. My soul is bourn up on his presence and my Heart is filled with His influence. How thankful ought we to be! How humble and submissive! Let us lay our heads on the pillow of peace and die peacefully in the embrace of God. (March 22, 1844; *Diary*, 164)

25

What the Lord will lead me to, for His presence is with me and directs my steps, what purpose of office of use however humble He may place me cannot be forseen. Oh Lord grant me humility patience peace and above all faith in thy ever-loving Kindness. Oh give me calmness restfulness in every trial of mind or body. (May 1, 1844; *Diary*, 173)

26

I feel very cheerful & at ease in perfect peace since I have consented to join the Catholic Church. Never have I felt the quietness the immovableness and the permanent rest that I now feel. It is inexpressible. I feel that essential and interior permanence which nothing exterior can disturb and that no act that it calls upon me to perform will in the

least cause me to be moved by it. It is with perfect
ease and gracefulness that I never dreamed of that
I will unite with the Church. It will not change but
fix my life. (June 13, 1844; *Diary*, 206)

27

Lord if I would could or should give myself
wholly up to Thee nothing but pure joy complete
happiness and exquisite pleasure would fill all my
Spirit Soul and Body. The Lord desires our whole
happiness: it is we who hinder him from causing
it to be so with our struggle against his Love
working Spirit. (June 14, 1844; *Diary*, 207–8)

28

Lord keep me ever in the permanent Love Spirit
substance and let me not descend otherwise than
in the Love Spirit in understanding & sense. Keep
me from all disputation and arguing. (June 14,
1844; *Diary*, 208)

29

Catholicism includes the positive in all faiths
ancient or modern, of profane or Christian sects.
(February 26, 1845; *Diary*, 292)

March

The Church

For Hecker, the spiritual search was never an end
in itself. The point of seeking was to find. Once
the object was found, the search ceased. Hecker
found fulfillment in the Catholic Church and
never regretted what he had found or desired to
look further. Rather, he desired to devote his life
to helping others—especially other seekers, such
as he himself had been—to find the truth in the
Catholic Church. Thus, all his activity after his conversion was characterized, above all, by his enthusiastic embrace of the Church to which his
personal spiritual search had so earnestly led him,
and which would in time transform him into an
active, enthusiastic missionary. Hecker's enthusiasm for his new faith and his commitment to the
Church permeate all his writings—from his initial
conversion experience as recorded in his diary,

through his active ministry as a priest and missionary preacher, to his final mature exposition in his last book, *The Church and the Age*.

That book is the source of many of the following reflections, as well as Hecker's monthly magazine, *The Catholic World*, and a collection of his sermons. One entry is from the diary he began in Egypt.

1

The Catholic Church alone seems to satisfy my wants my faith life soul....I may be laboring under a delusion; any thing you please. Yet my soul is Catholic and that faith...responds to my soul in its religious aspirations and its longings. I have not wished to make myself Catholic but it answers to the wants of my soul. It answers on all sides. It is so rich full. (April 24, 1843; *Diary*, 97)

2

The Catholic Church has preserved unity without encroachment on individual liberty and has preserved individual liberty without the loss of perfect unity. Unity without individual liberty is impossible as individual liberty is without unity.... It is only in Catholicism Unity and Individuality in divine unity that progress liberty and life is secured and perpetuated. (July 14, 1844; *Diary*, 220)

3

In all our reasoning we must understand that the criterion of truth is not the individual judgment of our personal Reason but the universal voice of the Catholic Church. Not that individual Reason is to be trusted in some case nor that it has not light, for the Voice of the Church is based upon the light of Reason, but it is this: the individual reason is not competent to comprehend the universal truth, hence no individual judgment is the criteria of absolute universal truth. (July 24, 1844; *Diary*, 226)

4

It never can be too often uttered that Catholicism means the Universal Good and True and Beautiful. That is not worthy to be named Catholicism which does not embrace all truth, all Goodness, all Beauty. Our allegiance is alone due to God and to Catholicism because it is the universal revelation of God. The measure of Catholicism is the measure of God's love to man. I am a Catholic because I would not reject any of God's Truth. (December 18, 1844; *Diary*, 279)

5

The doctrine of the infallibility of the Catholic Church is the only ground upon which there can possibly be any settledness and security in our faith. If the Church may err, if the Councils may err as undoubtedly individuals do then have we no surety of our faith and consequently of our salvation....The Church is the pillar and ground of truth. (July 4, 1845; *Diary*, 324)

6

Decree Nuper nonnulli releases Isaac Hecker and four companions from their Redemptorist vows, 1858

The Pope has spoken, and the American Fathers, including myself, are dispensed from their vows....The General is not mentioned in it, and no attention whatever is paid to his action in my regard. The other Fathers are dispensed in view of the petition they made...and in the dispensation I am associated with them....Now let us thank God for our success. (From a letter to the American Fathers, Rome, March 9, 1858; *PV*, 66)

7

Christianity, intelligibly understood, signifies the Church, the Catholic Church. The Church is God acting through a visible organization directly on men and, through men, on society. (*CA*, 22)

8

The Church is the sum of all problems, and the most potent fact in the whole universe. It is therefore illogical to look elsewhere for the radical remedy of all our evils. It is equally unworthy of a Catholic to look elsewhere for the renewal of religion. (*CA*, 22)

9

The Divine Spirit established the Church as the practical and perfect means of bringing all souls under His own immediate guidance and into complete union with God. This is the realization of the aim of all true religion. (*CA*, 38)

10

Thus all religions, as far as they contain truth and [are] viewed in the aspect of a divine life, find their common centre in the Catholic Church. (*CA*, 38)

11

The Church is God acting through the different races of men for their highest development, together with their present and future greatest happiness and His own greatest glory. "God directs the nations upon the earth" (Ps. 46:5). (*CA*, 41)

12

The perpetuity of the Catholic Church is placed above and beyond all dangers from any human or satanic conspiracies or attacks in that Divinity which is inherently incorporated with her existence, and in that invincible strength of conviction which this Divine Presence imparts to the souls of all her faithful children. (*CA*, 130)

13

The Catholic Church is the Church of God actualized upon earth so far as this is possible, human nature being what it is. (*CA*, 131)

14

But it would be absurd and an intolerable indignity for the soul to obey an authority that might lead it astray in a matter concerning its divine life and future destiny; for in the future world no liberty is left for a return to correct the mistakes into which the soul may have fallen. Therefore the claim is founded in right reason and justice that the supreme teaching and governing authority of the Church should be divine—that is, unerring. (*CA*, 136)

15

It is a fixed law, founded in the very nature of the Church, that every serious and persistent denial of a divinely revealed truth necessitates its vigorous defence, calls out its greater development, and ends, finally, in its dogmatic definition. (*CA*, 10)

16

For Christianity is the synthesis of all the scattered truths of every form of religion which has existed from the beginning of the world, and the Catholic Church is Christianity's complete, organic, living form. Christianity is the abstract expression of the Catholic Church, which, in the successive centuries of her existence, has come in contact with every race of men, and has known how to Christianize and retain them in her fold in harmony with their natural instincts. She has met humanity in every stage of its development...and, by working on the foundations of nature, she has captured them to the easy yoke of Christ. (*CA*, 157–58)

17

The Catholic faith rests upon three elementary facts—the competency of human reason, the infallibility of the Church, the veracity of God. He who undermines...one of these three positions destroys the Catholic faith. (*CA*, 213–14)

18

No other explanation of Christianity than the indwelling Christ in His Church as the actual and historical religion is tenable. (*CA*, 248)

19

Saint Joseph, Patron of the Universal Church

The life of St. Joseph is both interesting and instructive....What faith! What obedience! What disinterestedness!...He attained in society and in human relationships a degree of perfection not surpassed, if equaled, by the martyr's death, the contemplative of the solitude, the cloistered monk, or the missionary hero. ("The Saint of Our Day," *Sermons*, 100–101)

20

The most perfect criterion of certainty respecting matters of divine faith, the ordinary and the best means of attaining a reasonable and sure faith in revealed truths, is the authority of the Catholic

Church. God has made the church infallible, and has commanded us to hear and obey the church. In doing this he has acted according to the law which regulates the natural and the supernatural order. ("The Divine Authority of the Church," November 1885; CW, 161)

21

Facts and truths which are outside of the sphere of revelation and are purely objects of natural knowledge are not, as such, within the scope of the divine authority of the church, and cannot be defined, on their natural evidence, as dogmas of Catholic and divine faith. God has not made the church a medium for teaching in his name mathematics, physics, or history, and therefore has not given to her infallibility in respect to these matters, or any others in respect to which a similar reason runs. ("The Divine Authority of the Church," November 1885; CW, 163)

22

We know that by clearing the mind of doubt, by intensifying conviction into instinctive certitude, the divine authority in the church quickens the intellectual faculties into an activity whose liberty is altogether unknown to men outside her fold. And we know that the range of the soul's flight is and can only be infinitely widened by the working of an influence whose sole action is to attach the mind more and more firmly to an ever-widening...divine truth. ("The Human Environments of the Catholic Faith," July 1886; *CW*, 467)

23

You cannot solve the great problems of human destiny—problems which cannot be avoided—without accepting the mission of Christ and availing yourself of the Catholic Church. ("Dr. Brownson and Catholicity," November 1887; *CW*, 224)

24

Men are not one in organism, in society, as they are one in nature. Men are by nature organized into separate families and nations. To unite these families into one organism demands a more than natural bond, a supernatural authority. Unity is only maintained by the divine discipline of the Church....When, therefore, Jesus Christ became man and would embrace all men in one family, it followed that he must give us an organic life in addition to family and state. He did that in the Church. The Church is the inner and outer fellowship of all Christians under the perpetual authority of the apostolic office in the Papacy and the

episcope. ("The Things That Make for Unity,"
April 1888; CW, 106–7)

25
The Annunciation of the Lord

The Church is the substitute for the body of
Christ. Its continuance & expansion in time &
space. The Holy Spirit speaking by the mouths of
the prophets, *"locutus est per prophetas,"* prepared the way for the Incarnation; the Holy Spirit
prepared the body of Christ by overshadowing
the Blessed Virgin, *"adumbrabit tibi"*—The Holy
Spirit, after the death & ascension of Christ, came
down from above, *"descendit de coelis,"* and
established the Church. (Egypt, *PV*, 171)

26

Hence the Church of Christ, as an organism, is
the logical sequence of the Incarnation, and not
an accident or after-thought of Christ's mission to
men as their Mediator and Saviour. The Church
may justly be said to be the expansion, prolonga-
tion, and perpetuation of the Incarnation. Behold
the method by which Christ fulfils His promise to
remain upon earth unto the consummation of the
world! (*CA*, 248)

27

The Catholic idea, then, is this: that Christ, the only-begotten Son of God, has become man, and, after His ascension, continues His mission upon earth through the instrumentality of His Church as really and truly as when He was manifest in the flesh and walked among men, in the country about Judea. (*CA*, 249)

28

Hence the power and life of the Church can be no other than the indwelling Christ. As the soul is the life of the body, so Christ is the life of the Church. This is why St. Paul calls the Church "the Body of Christ." (*CA*, 250)

29

God, who made the rational soul, made also the material body, and it is the rational soul united to the material body that constitutes man, and that constituted the humanity of Christ. It is spirit and matter united by the authority of Christ that constitute a sacrament. The Incarnation is the universal sacrament from which Divine Source the specific sacraments derive their grace and efficacy. (*CA*, 251)

30

The realities which the Jewish ordinances fore-shadowed and promised the sacraments of the Church of Christ possess and bestow upon men. The sacraments, the Church, the Incarnation, and the twofold nature of man are all essentially inter-related. The Incarnation, the Church, and the sacraments rest upon the same foundation. (*CA*, 252)

31

Nothing less can satisfy the inmost desire of the soul, when once awakened, than truth in its wholeness and fulness. The mists of heresy are lifted up to make way for the glorious vision of the Church of the living God, the pillar and ground of truth. The winter is past, the spring has come, and the voice of the turtle-dove is heard in the land. (*CA*, 257)

April

The Church and the World

In nineteenth-century Europe, the Catholic Church was struggling to survive as an institution against an increasingly hostile political order. It sought to counteract the disruption associated with modern secularism and to reunite increasingly isolated individuals into a community by preserving, repairing, or restoring religious bonds. One way to do this was to assert the Church's claims to authority as vigorously as possible and to insist upon political privileges and institutional rights in relation to the state. For Hecker, the American experience suggested a more promising alternative approach, which recognized, accommodated, and, to some extent, celebrated the separate but converging spheres of the spiritual and the temporal, religion and society, church and state.

The reflections for this month are from *The Church and the Age*, the magazine *The Catholic World*, *The Paulist Vocation*, and a larger sampling of Hecker's sermons.

1

I have nothing to do with those causes which lie in the mercantile or political world; for the sanctuary is not the place for the discussion of these questions. Our duty here is to deal with man in his religious nature, in his relations with God. ("How to Be Happy," *Sermons*, 59)

2

If you mean...that the earth is hateful and the world nothing but sin; that the soul is wholly depraved, and life is only another word for misery; then we reply, no; a thousand times, no! The Gospel we preach is not one of gloom and despair, but of glad tidings and great joy. The Creed we hold teaches us to "believe in God the Father Almighty, the Creator of Heaven and Earth, and all things visible and invisible." ("How to Be Happy," *Sermons*, 60)

3

We protest, therefore, against the idea of giving the earth over to wretchedness and the world to sin; rather would we indulge the hope of establishing God's kingdom here, and labor earnestly for it. ("How to Be Happy," *Sermons*, 60–61)

4

There is little or no hope at all of our entering into the kingdom of heaven hereafter, if we are not citizens of it here. ("How to Be Happy," *Sermons*, 61)

5

Beauty, Holiness, and Goodness, the contemplation of which filled and nourished the souls of the saints upon earth, in what does it differ from the source of their happiness in heaven? There is no difference except that here we see obscurely by the light of faith, there we shall see clearly, face to face, by the light of glory. The object of happiness then upon earth is the same as in heaven; the soul too will exercise the same faculties in both places. The actual life, therefore, of a true Christian upon earth, is a participation in the happiness of the kingdom of heaven. ("How to Be Happy," *Sermons*, 62)

6

The aim, then, of the Gospel is not to separate heaven from earth, or the earth from heaven, or to place between them an antagonism; the object of the Gospel is to bring them together, unite them and make them one; briefly, to establish the reign of God "upon earth as it is in heaven." ("How to Be Happy," *Sermons*, 62)

7

Compulsion never gave birth to faith which is "not, by any means, a blind assent of the mind" [First Vatican Council] but essentially an intelligent and voluntary act. Convinced of this, as Catholics, the idea of religious tolerance flowed naturally and consistently in the minds of the first settlers on the shores of the Potomac. It was a noble act on their part to proclaim that within the province and jurisdiction of Maryland, no Christian man should be molested in worshipping God according to the dictates of his conscience. (*CA*, 66)

8

The Creator invested man with these [natural] rights in order that he might fulfil the duties inseparably attached to them. For these rights put man in the possession of himself, and leave him free to reach the end for which his Creator called him into existence. He, therefore, who denies or violates these rights offends God, acts the tyrant, and is an enemy of mankind. (*CA*, 69)

9

Since Christianity claims to be God's revelation of the great end for which He created man, it follows that those rights without which [man] cannot reach that end must find their sanction, expressed or implied, in all true interpretations of its doctrines. (*CA*, 69)

10

The Catholic Church has flourished under all forms of government. Her Divine Founder has given her an organism capable of adjustment to every legitimate human institution. She tends to make the people loyal to the reasonable authority of the state, and her influence will strengthen them in the virtues necessary for the public welfare; it has always done so. (*CA*, 105–6)

11

The Church has plainly shown in ages past that she can live and gain the empire over souls, even against the accumulated power of a hostile and persecuting state. She has shown in modern times, both in the United States and in England and

Ireland, that independent of the state, and [independent] of all other support than the voluntary offerings of her children, even with stinted freedom, she can maintain her independence, grow strong and prosperous. (*CA*, 144)

12

The Catholic Church teaches to men their true relations to God and to their fellow-men, and by the practical application of the principles which govern these relations are removed the errors and vices which hinder the establishment of the reign of God in men's souls and everywhere upon earth. (*CA*, 163)

13

Make a list of all the honest demands for ameliorations and reforms in man's social, industrial, and political condition—it will not be a short one—and you will discover that they have their truth in the Spirit, and are justified by the teachings and the practice of the Catholic Church. (*CA*, 167)

14

The phase of Catholicity which is now coming slowly to the light will gather up all the rich treasures of the past, march in response to every honest demand of the interests of the actual present, and guide the genuine aspirations of the race in the sure way to the more perfect future of its hopes. (*CA*, 168)

15

This sublime mission is not the self-imposed work of any man or party of men, but the divinely imposed task of religion, of the present, visible, living body of Christ, the Church of God. None other has the power to renew the world, unite together in one band the whole human race, and direct its energies to enterprises worthy of man's great destiny. (*CA*, 168)

16

None recognize the divine origin of the state more strenuously and sincerely than Catholics. Catholics are not, and never were, in favor of theocracy—the absorption of the functions of the state into the Church—that is a Puritan idea; nor are they in favor of the abolition of the state—that is a communistic dream. ("The German Problem," December 1881; *CW*, 291)

17

History teaches indisputably that the church can exist independently of the state much better than the state can exist independently of the church. Is it not a sign of a lack of faith, and an injustice to the divine character of the church, to mistrust her ability to stand upon her own feet and maintain herself erect? ("The German Problem," December 1881; *CW*, 296)

18

It is when both church and state are the expressions of the religious faith and political convictions of the entire community, and each acts in its own sphere concordantly with the other in aiding man to attain his divinely appointed destiny, that the kingdom of God upon earth approaches its nearest fulfilment. ("The German Problem," December 1881; *CW*, 296)

19

Now that the old system between church and state has been broken, and its recovery hopeless, may it not be the interest no less than the policy of the church not to neglect but to embrace the opportunity which Heaven yields to secure above all things, in view of menacing dangers, her independence and freedom of action? ("The German Problem," December 1881; *CW*, 296–97)

20

For Christianity means this: to raise men above themselves, above human nature, above the ties of family, above the ties which bind them to a nation or to a race; but not condemning or sundering these, but renewing them, and communicating and establishing them at the same time in the tie of filial relations with God, and in this Christ-given tie to unite all men in a common but higher than a natural brotherhood. ("The American Congress of Churches," December 1885; *CW*, 413)

21

Practical men will be attracted to that form of Christianity in which they perceive doctrines and an organism which are an exhaustless reservoir of the very element which is an essential requirement of a free and great people. Whatever can unite the children of every race into one brotherhood, by methods at once of divine origin and representative of the people, cannot fail to elicit the admiration of men whose ambition is to live in a commonwealth as vast as it is free. This will be especially the case with men who seek the public good from motives of religion and philanthropy. ("Baptized Democracy," September 1886; *CW*, 726)

22

Democracy is founded on the natural brotherhood of men. Catholicity is founded on a higher brotherhood than that of nature; it is given us through the divinity of Christ. The first leads up to the second, and [only by it can] best secure its results. The Catholic Church contains the ideal of the democracy, and in the long run will be found necessary as well for its preservation as for its continued advance towards perfect human brotherhood. ("Baptized Democracy," September 1886; CW, 727)

23

It is ourselves that we have to liberalize, and not our Catholicity; and to liberalize ourselves by the development and maximizing of Catholicity within us and around us. ("Baptized Democracy," September 1886; CW, 729)

24

It is astonishing how much more liberal the Catholic religion is than Catholic people. Where is the Catholic man who will say that he is as liberal as his religion? The highest encomium that can be passed on a man is to say that he is as broad as the doctrines the Catholic Church teaches. ("Baptized Democracy," September 1886; CW, 729)

25

Is not the triumph of religion more complete & beautiful when united with an enlightened intelligence, and embraced by a free & undivided world? Is it bold to say that Religion, thus combined with intelligence & freedom, promises to

furnish the world with a more advanced &
Christian civilization? ("The Present and Future
Prospects of the Catholic Faith in the United
States of North America," December 1857–
January 1858; in *PV*, 267)

26

Again, the more energetic & naturally gifted a
people, the more grand under the influence of
divine grace will be their destiny; for grace does
not set aside, but answers, purifies, elevates &
invigorates nature. The authority of the Church
does not suppress the liberty of the will, but
directs it, enlarges its sphere of action, & consecrates its activity to noble enterprises. ("The
Present and Future Prospects of the Catholic Faith
in the United States of North America,"
December 1857–January 1858; in *PV*, 268)

27

The tree of Catholicity grows strong and bears
precious fruit when planted in the soil of liberty
and intelligence. Would to God that the Catholic
Church everywhere in Europe enjoyed liberty to
preach her holy faith and exercise her salutary
discipline, as she does in the United States!
Religion reigns most worthily, in an age tempered
like ours, when she rules by the voluntary force of

the intelligent convictions of conscience, and finds in these alone her sufficient support. ("The German Problem," December 1881; *CW*, 296)

28

For scarcely anyone who has made this subject a serious study, will pretend that an entire separation of Church and State can be maintained, were it possible, as the normal and more perfect condition of society. It is a truth established by the best of ancient and modern writers of all schools, on the philosophy of political governments, that religion is the basis of all society, and its dogmas the foundation of political principles. Sooner or later an intelligent people must recognize this connection. (From a letter to Brownson, January 30, 1870; *BH*, 281)

29

Every day my admiration increases at the attitude of the Holy Father [Bl. Pius IX] in his defense of those principles which underlie the political order and natural morality....He is resisting the destruction of all human society. [He is] the only power on earth that has had the courage to stand up against violence and injustice in the political order. Wonderful mission for God's Church! (From a letter to Brownson, April 3, 1871; *BH*, 302)

30

An old priest of my acquaintance once said...that he didn't care for union of church and state if he could have union of church and people. A very wise remark, and a solution of a difficult question, but it can apply only under a popular government. ("The Mission of Leo XIII," October 1888; CW, 9)

May

Contemporary Holiness: The Church and the Modern Age

In his preaching and writing, Isaac Hecker self-consciously sought and promoted images and models of holiness that he believed resonated well within the new context created by what he saw happening in the modern world. An excellent example of this is his often-quoted 1863 sermon on Saint Joseph, "The Saint of Our Day." Consistent with his theology of the Church and his understanding of the role of free individuals in modern society, he constantly sought to promote an understanding of and devotion to the Church that would be consistent with the kind of contemporary holiness he believed most relevant for the circumstances of the modern age.

The selections for this month are primarily from the sermon "The Saint of Our Day" and from *The Church and the Age.*

1
Saint Joseph the Worker

Our age lives in its busy marts, in counting-rooms, in work-shops, in homes, and in the varied relations that form human society, and it is into these that sanctity is to be introduced. St. Joseph stands forth as an excellent and unsurpassed model of this type of perfection. ("The Saint of Our Day," *Sermons,* 102)

2

Every age has its own characteristics. It is this that gives a peculiar expression to every form of its life, whether it be in art, science, or politics.... Now this law also holds in the history of religion. Every age of the Church has its own characteristic form of expression. There is something about the sanctity of each age peculiar to itself. ("The Saint of Our Day," *Sermons,* 91)

3

Thus we see that every age has had a type of sanctity peculiar to itself. An age of heathen persecution against the holy faith gave to Christian heroism the form of martyrdom. A degraded society peopled the solitudes of the deserts, and caused them to blossom with the flowers of sublime Christian virtues. Against the rudeness of barbarism were raised the cloistered walls of monasteries and convents, alike schools of learning and Christian perfection. The religious revolution of the sixteenth century called out an army of defenders of the faith and heroic missionaries. ("The Saint of Our Day," *Sermons*, 95–96)

4

Each type or form of sanctity differed in its expression from the other. Each class of men did in their day what their age required. Each was true to its time, its wants, its promises, and therefore had its peculiar charm and beauty. ("The Saint of Our Day," *Sermons*, 96)

5

It is likewise a monstrous tyranny of opinion to arraign the past, judge and condemn it, by the standards of the present; and we resist it with no less energy than the spirit that would mould the slips of the present into the antiquated forms of bygone ages. ("The Saint of Our Day," *Sermons*, 97)

6

The Catholic Church, like all that is divine, is ever ancient and ever new, "and the same for ever." Her mission is to guide man to the realization of the great end of his being, and for this purpose her Divine Founder has furnished her with full and adequate means for all men, for all ages, unto the consummation of time. ("The Saint of Our Day," *Sermons*, 97)

7

[The nineteenth century] claims to be a period of most advanced civilization; to be marked by unprecedented diffusion of intelligence and liberty. So far as the claims are true, so far you have the indication of what the people of the age will be when their intelligence and liberty are completely dedicated to God. ("The Saint of Our Day," *Sermons*, 97)

8

The more a civilization solicits the exercise of man's intelligence, and enlarges the field for the action of his free-will, the broader will be the basis that it offers for sanctity. Ignorance and weakness are the negation of life; they are either sinful or the consequences of sin, and to remedy these common evils is the aim of the Christian religion. Enlightened intelligence and true liberty of the will are essential conditions of all moral actions, and the measure of their merit. ("The Saint of Our Day," *Sermons*, 98)

9

The true development of sanctity in the saint, will be in measure to the extent of the true enlightenment of the intelligence, and the right exercise of the will. A defective knowledge and a restricted freedom produce only an incomplete development of sanctity. ("The Saint of Our Day," *Sermons*, 99)

10

The ideal of true Christian perfection is the union of religion with a fully enlightened intelligence, and an entire liberty of will, directed wholly to the realization of the great end of our being. ("The Saint of Our Day," *Sermons*, 99)

11

Christianity is designed for the sanctification of our whole nature, with all its faculties, powers, and propensities, since it was the entire and complete manhood that was united to the Godhead in Christ; we affirm, therefore, that the more advanced and complete a civilization, the wider will be the sphere for the display of its divine character. ("The Saint of Our Day," *Sermons*, 99–100)

12

Religion has nothing to fear from the "uncoverings of science"; for these will not prove in opposition to her divinely revealed truths, nor identical with them, but will only serve to show more clearly their divine character and origin and their necessity. ("The Saint of Our Day," *Sermons*, 100)

13

The ideal of Catholicity is the union of religion with intelligence and liberty in all their completeness. Man renders to God that perfect worship when he offers the homage of his entire intelligence and liberty. ("The Saint of Our Day," *Sermons*, 100)

14

For it is the difficulties and hindrances that Christians find in their age which give the form to their character and habits, and when mastered, become the means of divine grace and their titles of glory. Indicate these, and you portray that type of sanctity in which the life of the Church will find its actual and living expression. ("The Saint of Our Day," *Sermons*, 102)

15

Religion is the solution to the problem of man's destiny. Religion, therefore, lies at the root of everything which concern's man's true interest. (*CA*, 22)

16

The greater part of the intellectual errors of the age arise from a lack of knowledge of the essential relations of the light of faith with the light of reason; of the connection between the mysteries and truths of divine revelation and those discovered and attainable by human reason; of the action of divine grace and the action of the human will. (*CA*, 38)

17

For God is no less the author of nature than of grace, of reason than of faith, of this earth than of heaven. (*CA*, 60)

18

Isaac and George Hecker are confirmed, New York, Trinity Sunday, 1845

The Word by which all things were made that were made, and the Word which was made flesh, is one and the same Word. The light which enlighteneth every man that cometh into this world, and the light of Christian faith, are, although different in degree, the same light. "There is therefore nothing so foolish or so absurd," to use the words of Pius IX on the same subject, "as to suppose there can be any opposition between them." (*CA*, 60–61)

19

For what else did Christ become man than to establish the kingdom of God on earth as the way to the kingdom of God in heaven? (*CA*, 61)

20

Every religious dogma has a special bearing on political society, and this bearing is what constitutes its political principle; and every political principle has a religious bearing, and this bearing involves a religious dogma which is its premise. (*CA*, 79)

21

It cannot be too often repeated to the men of this generation, so many of whom are trying to banish and forget God, that God, and God alone, is the Creator and Renewer of the world. The same God who made all things, and who became man, and began the work of regeneration, is the same who really acts in the Church now upon men and society, and who has pledged His word to continue to do so until the end of the world. (*CA*, 61)

22

The human mind was made by its Creator for truth, and in the absence of truth it ceases to live. When it refuses its assent to truth it is either because the truth has been travestied and made to appear false, or because it is seen through a distorted medium. For the intellect is powerless to reject the truth...except by committing a crime against itself. It is not in the search after truth, but in the tranquil possession of truth and appropriation of it by contemplation, that man finds the fullest and purest joy. (*CA*, 94–95)

23

Nor is it a question as to whether the Church will be reconciled with modern civilization. The real question is whether modern society will follow the principles of eternal justice and right, and reject false teachers; whether it will legislate in accordance with the rules of right reason and the divine truths of Christianity, and turn its back upon revolution, anarchy, and atheism; whether it will act in harmony with God's Church in upholding modern civilization and in spreading God's kingdom upon earth, or return to paganism, barbarism, and savagery. (*CA*, 132)

24

There were special causes which made it reasonable that the occupant of St. Peter's chair at Rome should in modern times be an Italian. Owing to the radical changes which have taken place in Europe, these causes no longer have the force they once had. The Church is a universal, not a national society....The Supreme Pastor of the whole flock of Christ, as befits the Catholic and cosmopolitan spirit of the Church, may now, as in former days, be chosen solely in view of his capacity, fitness, and personal merits, without any regard to his nationality or race. (*CA*, 139–40)

25

The order and stability of modern society and civilization are based upon the truths which find their root and support in the doctrines unswervingly taught and uncompromisingly upheld by the Catholic Church. Among these great truths are the divinity of Christ and the divine establishment and perpetuity of his Church upon earth; the unquestionable responsibility of both kings and peoples to the law of God; the indissolubility of the marriage tie and the sacredness of the family;

the reign of the law of justice between man and man, and, when violated, the strict obligation of restitution; the sacredness of oaths and the equality of all men, without distinction of rank, color, or race, before God. (*CA*, 150)

26
St. Philip Neri

The conception of a movement of the nature of the Paulists was one which preoccupied my mind a long while. It was of a community in which the elements of self-control, conscience, and the internal guidance of the Holy Spirit should take the lead, and should be relied on for attaining perfection more than the control of discipline, rules, and external authority. The result would be a type of perfection more in accordance with that of St. Philip Neri than with that of St. Ignatius. (*PV*, 126–27)

27

That religious motives to an almost incredible extent have become extinct in some men's souls we, with pain and pity, admit; that this is the case with the bulk of mankind is an egregious mistake. There has seldom been an age when religious questions occupied so large a share of intellectual attention as our own; and religious motives still influence the bulk of mankind in their conduct. (*CA*, 155)

28

It is through the faithful reception of the divine action of the Catholic Church by individuals and society that the highest good possible for man here and hereafter can be surely attained; and this needs only clearly to be seen to restore to her true and visible fold all the descendants of the members separated from the Catholic Church by the religious revolution of the sixteenth century, at least all who are in good faith. (*CA*, 164–65)

29

For the object of Christ in the Church is not to interpose the Church, or her sacraments, or her worship between Himself and the soul, but through their instrumentality to come in personal contact with the soul, and by the power of His grace to wash away its sins, communicate to it sonship with God as the heavenly Father, and thereby to satisfy it. (*CA*, 250)

30

When the Church is spoken of as an object in itself to be upheld & glorified, instead of a means to an end, we misplace it, and many minds are misled, and antipathies and resistance are created when this might & should be avoided, and thus with the best intentions the Church and souls are injured, the very cause at heart is hindered. (Egypt, *PV*, 171)

31

To send a man back eighteen centuries, or to tell him to read a book, however good, when he feels the pressing need of the love of the infinite God in his heart, is downright mockery. If Christ is to be to us a savior, we must find him here, now, and where we are, in this age of ours also; otherwise he is no Christ, no Saviour, no Immanuel, no "God with us." (*The Paulist Prayer Book*, 217–18)

June

The Holy Spirit and the Individual

In the first period of Hecker's life, animated by a self-conscious appreciation of God's Providence, he had discerned the presence and action of the Holy Spirit in God's providential care for him and had identified his own inner aspirations and longings with the action of the indwelling Holy Spirit. Thereafter, one of his strikingly distinctive emphases as a Catholic—in his own personal spiritual life, in his reflections regarding his Paulist religious community, and in his general spiritual teaching—would be his intense personal devotion to the Holy Spirit and his desire to foster among the faithful an increased appreciation of, and openness to, the fundamental activity and inspiration of the Holy Spirit operating in each individual.

The selections for this month come largely from *The Church and the Age*, *The Paulist Vocation*, and Hecker's diary begun in Egypt.

1

[I have] entire faith in the personal guidance of the Holy Spirit, and complete confidence in its action in all things—in its infinite love, wisdom, power; that it is under its influence and promptings up to now my life has been led. Though not clearly seen or known, He has directed every step. On this faith, on this principle, promised to act now and in time to come. To be above fear, doubt, hesitation, or timidity, but patient, obedient, and stable. (From private memoranda made in Europe during his illness, *PV*, 90)

2

The work of the Holy Ghost began on the day of Pentecost, when He descended visibly to the Apostles and disciples. It is in this dispensation we live, and when He reigns on earth, the work of the Holy Spirit will be finished. When is realized the petition of the Saviour, "Thy will be done on earth as it is in heaven." (Notes on the Holy Spirit, *PV*, 176–77)

3

Through the Holy Spirit the world was called out of chaos. Through Him the patriarchs and prophets were inspired. Through Him the way to the Incarnation was prepared. Through Him the Church was established. Through Him every Christian soul is regenerated. Through Him all things receive their perfection and are glorified. (Notes on the Holy Spirit, *PV*, 177)

4

Through the Holy Spirit the martyrs received the strength to sustain triumphantly their sufferings. Through Him the apostles of nations were filled with zeal and power to convert nations. Through Him the innumerable litany of the Saints were sanctified. Through the Holy Spirit we receive all that is Holy, Good, True and Beautiful. (Notes on the Holy Spirit, *PV*, 177)

5

Sanctity is the result of the primary or immediate action of the Holy Spirit in the individual soul and its faithful correspondence with this inspiration. (Notes on the Holy Spirit, *PV*, 177)

6

The essential and universal principle which saves and sanctifies the soul is the Holy Spirit. He it was who called, inspired, and sanctified the patriarchs, the prophets and saints of the old dispensation. The same Divine Spirit inspired and sanctified the apostles, the martyrs, and the saints of the new dispensation. (*CA*, 23–24)

7

The actual and habitual guidance of the soul by the Holy Spirit is the essential principle of all divine life....Christ's mission was to give the Holy Spirit more abundantly. (*CA*, 24)

8

In accordance with the Sacred Scriptures, the Catholic Church teaches that the Holy Spirit is infused, with all his gifts, into our souls by the sacrament of baptism, and that without His actual prompting or inspiration, and aid, no thought or act or even wish, tending directly towards our true destiny, is possible. (*CA*, 25)

9

The whole aim of the science of Christian perfection is to instruct men how to remove the hindrances in the way of the action of the Holy

Spirit, and how to cultivate those virtues which are most favorable to His solicitations and inspirations. (*CA*, 25)

10

Thus the sum of spiritual life consists in observing and yielding to the movements of the Spirit of God in our soul, employing for this purpose all the exercises of prayer, spiritual reading, sacraments, the practice of virtues, and good works. (*CA*, 25)

11

That divine action which is the immediate and principal cause of the salvation and perfection of the soul claims by right its direct and main attention. From this source within the soul there will gradually come to birth the consciousness of the indwelling presence of the Holy Spirit, out of which will spring a force surpassing all human strength, a courage higher than all human heroism, a sense of dignity excelling all human greatness. The light the age requires for its renewal can come only from the same source. (*CA*, 25–26)

12

The practical aim of all true religion is to bring each individual soul under the immediate guidance of the Divine Spirit. (*CA*, 37)

13

The Divine Spirit acts as the principle of regeneration and sanctification in each Christian soul. (*CA*, 37)

14

Let each soul study the way in which the Holy Ghost attracts it, be faithful to that...& not depart on any account from it. (From a letter to Mrs. King, March 25, 1863; *PV*, 168)

15

In proportion as the Holy Spirit takes possession and direction of our soul will our intelligence increase in light (Jn. 16:13), our hearts in love, and our will in liberty (2 Cor. 3:17); action, humility, obedience and every virtue will be practiced. (Notes on the Holy Spirit, *PV*, 175)

16

Not an anxious search, least of all a craving for extraordinary lights; but a constant readiness to perceive the divine guidance in the secret ways of the soul, and then to act with decision and a noble and generous courage—this is true wisdom. (On the guidance of the Holy Spirit, *PV*, 131)

17

Not to "resist the Spirit" is the first duty. Fidelity to the divine guidance, yielding one's self up lovingly to the impulses of virtue as they gently claim control of our thoughts—this is the simple duty. (On the guidance of the Holy Spirit, *PV*, 132)

18

The end of all spiritual exercises is to place the soul in those dispositions which are most favorable to bring down upon it the grace of God and place it under the guidance of His Holy Spirit. ("Thoughts on the Spiritual Life," 1865; *PV*, 213)

19

But this bringing our entire nature with all its propensities & passions under the entire guidance of the Holy Ghost is a great work. It is great in its end, painful, mysterious, dreadful in its operations. Few have any conception of it. Others seem not to have the capacities to conceive even what it is. Many live years and years in religion and do not dream of it. Some see it for a time & aim at it, but from willfulness shut it out of sight again. Some begin, advance, but fail for want of courage. (*PV*, 213)

20

It is no small task indeed to bring all our thoughts, affections & actions & expressions in accordance with the dictates of the Holy Ghost. How few know what it means to give oneself wholly, & unreservedly, to God & persist unto the end in not withstraining anything of this gift again. (*PV*, 213–14)

21

The indwelling Divine Presence is the key to the Catholic position, and they who cannot perceive and appreciate this, whatever may be their grasp of intellect or the extent of their knowledge, will find themselves baffled in attempting to explain her existence and history. (*CA*, 131)

22

It is the birthright of every member of the Catholic Church freely to follow the promptings of the Holy Spirit, and the office and aim of the authority of the Church is to secure, defend, and protect this Christ-given freedom. (*CA*, 135)

23

The individuality of a man cannot be too strong or his liberty too great when he is guided by the Spirit of God. But when these are interpreted as independency from God and license, when impressions are taken too easily from below, instead of those from above, then this is evidence of the spirit of pride and of the flesh, and not of "the liberty of the glory of the children of God." (*PV*, 185)

24
Birth of Saint John the Baptist

We have much to learn before we know all that union with God means, all that loneliness demands, all that Man is. Alas how few live solely for God—Mary—John the Baptist—these from their birth were consecrated to his work alone. (April 2, 1845; *Diary*, 296)

25

The Catholic idea of Christian perfection as a system is built up, in all its minute parts, upon the central conception of the immediate guidance of the soul by the indwelling Holy Spirit. The Catholic Church teaches that the Holy Spirit is infused into the souls of men, accompanied with His heavenly gifts, by the instrumentality of the sacrament of baptism. (*CA*, 218)

26

Thus a man becomes a child of God, according to the teaching of Christ, not by right of birth, but by the grace of baptism. By the creative act man is made a creature of God; by the indwelling presence of the Holy Spirit man is made a Christian. (*CA*, 218)

27

The Holy Spirit, having taken up His abode in the Christian soul and become its abiding guest, enlightens, quickens, and strengthens it to run in the way of perfection. (*CA*, 218)

28

By the practice of recollection, prayer, fidelity to divine inspirations, moved and aided by the gifts of the Holy Spirit, [Christian souls] render the dictates of reason submissive, pliant, and docile to the teachings and guidance of the Holy Spirit, until this becomes a habit and, as it were, spontaneous. Thus Christian souls, by the interior action of the Holy Spirit, attain perfection—that is, become divine men! This is the ideal Christian man, the saint! (*CA*, 219)

29
Solemnity of Saints Peter and Paul

The great apostles, St. Peter and St. Paul, did not stop in Jerusalem, but turned their eyes and steps towards all-conquering, all-powerful Rome. Their faith and their heroism, sealed with their martyrdom, after a long and bloody contest, obtained the victory. The imperial Roman eagles became proud to carry aloft the victorious cross of Christ! (*CA*, 52)

30
First Martyrs of the Church of Rome

What we need to-day is men whose spirit is that of the early martyrs. We shall get them in proportion as Catholics cultivate a spirit of independence and personal conviction. The highest development of religion in the soul is when it is assisted by free contemplation of the ultimate causes of things. Intelligence and liberty are the human environments most favorable to the deepening of personal conviction of religious truth and obedience to the interior movements of an enlightened conscience. (*CA*, 108)

July

The Holy Spirit and the Church

For all his American individualism, Isaac Hecker categorically rejected what he saw as the fragmented character of American Protestantism, and, accordingly, came to appreciate the ministry of authority in the Catholic Church, in which he recognized a divinely sanctioned providential alternative to the principle of individual interpretation. In the internal order and structure of the visible, institutional Church; in its sacramental system; and in its various historical structures (in particular, the rich heritage of its different religious communities)—Hecker recognized the divinely sanctioned means for the fulfillment of Christ's life and mission on earth, pouring the oil of the Holy Spirit on the troubled waters of the world.

Most of the selections for this month are from *The Church and the Age*, *The Paulist Vocation*, and Hecker's diary begun in Egypt.

1

Christ came to introduce that pure excitement which should become permanent in humanity and place us in rapport with the unseen to us as we naturally are. The Church is the means by which we are put in rapport with Christ, God, the Holy Ghost. (July 27, 1844; *Diary*, 230–31)

2

The wind is the Holy Spirit—the North star is the eternal authority of the Church, the compass is the light of faith. (Egypt, *PV*, 170)

3

To wish to enlarge the action of the Holy Spirit in the Soul, independently of, or without the knowledge & appreciation of the necessity of the external authority of the Church—her discipline, her laws, her worship, etc. & the spirit of obedience—would only be opening the door to eccentricity, schism, heresy, & spiritual death. (Egypt, *PV*, 170)

4

He who does not see the external authority of the Church, and the internal action of the Holy Spirit in an inseparable synthesis, has not a right or just conception of either. (Egypt, *PV*, 170)

5

To view the external authority, discipline, etc. of the Church independently of its purpose, & without appreciation of that purpose—which is to communicate the Divine Spirit to the soul, & to perfect it by the operations of that Spirit—is to make religion a formality & [a] mechanism, dry & irksome, creating a dislike, destructive of liberty, manliness & sanctity. (Egypt, *PV*, 170–71)

6

Suppose the time has come for a greater effusion of the Holy Spirit in the Church & her members, and thus a great increase of the sanctity with all that flows from sanctity takes place, will not this be the means best adapted, most efficacious in the conversion of those races which are not yet Christians? (Egypt, *PV*, 171)

7

Isaac Hecker and three companions form the Paulist Fathers, 1858

The main purpose of each Paulist must be the attainment of personal perfection by the practice of those virtues without which it cannot be secured—mortification, self-denial, detachment, and the like. By the use of these means the grace of God makes the soul perfect. The perfect soul is one which is guided instinctively by the indwelling Holy Spirit. To attain to this is the end always to be aimed at in the practice of the virtues just named. ("Personal Sanctification of the Paulist and His Standard of Perfection," in *PV*, 124–25)

8

The pages of the history of the Church teach that in every age she has had her saints and providential men. But in addition to these, at the beginning of every important or critical epoch, the Holy Spirit has called into existence Religious Institutions. The aim of these institutions, appreciating the aspirations and understanding the errors of their day, and guided by the instinct of divine grace, was to establish religious organizations fitted to direct aright the one and to refute the other. ("On the Mission of New Religious Communities," in *PV*, 285–86)

9

The essential element of all religious organizations, it is well to know, has always been the same: a special inspiration of the Holy Spirit. Their peculiar form depends upon the particular needs of the Church and society at the time when they are called into existence. ("On the Mission of New Religious Communities," in *PV*, 286)

10

This is the explanation of the origin and different characteristics of all the great Religious Orders of the Church....Each was inspired by the Holy Spirit to do the special work which had to be done in its own day. ("On the Mission of New Religious Communities," in *PV*, 286–87)

11

Saint Benedict

St. Benedict did not plunge into solitude...but founded a religious community fitted to meet the great needs of the fifth century. ("On the Mission of New Religious Communities," in *PV*, 286). In the consecrated walls of monasteries and cloisters were nurtured a multitude of souls who sought in these retreats to satisfy the yearnings of their religious nature, which the world around them afforded not the means of doing. ("The Saint of Our Day," *Sermons*, 93)

12

The great work of the Holy Spirit is the salvation, the sanctification of mankind upon earth and their glorification hereafter *by means* of the Church. (Egypt, *PV*, 171)

13

By the authority of the Church the Holy Spirit is the teacher & criterion of Truth. Through the Sacraments He communicates Himself to the soul, according to its peculiar needs. By the worship of the Church He adores and gives expression to the religious life of the soul. By its discipline He is the guardian of the divine life of the soul. The Church is therefore the organ by which the work of man's redemption, begun by Christ on earth, is continued & completed. (Egypt, *PV*, 171–72)

14

It is the Holy Spirit who, through the sacrament of ordination, is in the priest who consecrates the Body and Blood of Christ, who pardons sins, who blesses, teaches the word of God, and dispenses grace. Not the man. *Sacerdos est alter Christus* ("The priest is another Christ"). It is the Holy Spirit who teaches and judges in the head of the

Church. *Christus locutus est per papam* ("Christ speaks through the pope"). The Holy Spirit is therefore the soul, life, indwelling in the Church. (Egypt, *PV*, 172)

15

It cannot be too deeply and firmly impressed on the mind that the Church is actuated by the instinct of the Holy Spirit, and to discern clearly its action, and to co-operate with it effectually, is the highest employment of our faculties, and at the same time the primary source of the greatest good to society. (*CA*, 23)

16

Did we clearly see and understand the divine action of the Holy Spirit in the successive steps of the history of the Church, we should fully comprehend the law of all true progress. (*CA*, 23)

17

The Holy Spirit established the Church, and can He forget His own mission? It is true that He has to guide and govern through men, but He is the sovereign of men, and especially of those whom he has chosen as His immediate instruments. (*CA*, 23)

18

For the definition of the [First] Vatican Council, having rendered the supreme authority of the Church, which is the unerring interpreter and criterion of divinely revealed truth, more explicit and complete, has prepared the way for the faithful to follow, with greater safety and liberty, the inspirations of the Holy Spirit. (*CA*, 29)

19

The exclusive view of the external authority of the Church, without a proper understanding of the nature and work of the Holy Spirit in the soul, would render the practice of religion formal, obedience servile, and the Church sterile. (*CA*, 33)

20

The action of the Holy Spirit embodied visibly in the authority of the Church, and the action of the Holy Spirit dwelling invisibly in the soul, form one inseparable synthesis. (*CA*, 33)

21

The Holy Spirit, in the external authority of the Church, acts as the infallible interpreter and criterion of divine revelation. The Holy Spirit in the soul acts as the Divine Life Giver and Sanctifier. It is of the highest importance that these two distinct offices of the Holy Spirit should not be confounded. (*CA*, 34)

22

The Holy Spirit, which, through the authority of the Church, teaches divine truth, is the same Spirit which prompts the soul to receive the divine truths which He teaches. The measure of our love for the Holy Spirit is the measure of our obedience to the authority of the Church; and the measure of our obedience to the authority of the Church is the measure of our love for the Holy Spirit. (*CA*, 34)

23

In case of obscurity or doubt concerning what is the divinely revealed truth, or whether what prompts the soul is or is not an inspiration of the Holy Spirit, recourse must be had to the divine teacher or criterion, the authority of the Church....The test, therefore, of a truly enlightened and sincere Christian will be, in case of uncertainty, the promptitude of his obedience to the voice of the Church. (*CA*, 35)

24

It is the divine action of the Holy Spirit in and through the Church which gives her external organization the reason for its existence. And it is the fuller explanation of the divine side of the Church and its relations with her human side, giving always to the former its due accentuation, that will contribute to the increase of the interior life of the faithful, and aid powerfully to remove the blindness of those, whose number is much larger than is commonly supposed, who only see the Church on her human side. (*CA*, 37)

25

The Divine Spirit communicates Himself to the soul by means of the sacraments of the Church. The Divine Spirit acts as the interpreter and criterion of revealed truth by the authority of the Church. (*CA*, 37)

26

The same Spirit clothes with suitable ceremonies and words the truths of religion, and the interior life of the soul, in the liturgy and devotions of the Church. The Divine Spirit acts as the safeguard of the life of the soul and of the household of God in the discipline of the Church. (*CA*, 37–38)

27

The Holy Spirit, of which the Church is the organ and expression, places every soul, and therefore all nations and races, in the immediate and perfect relation with their supreme end, God, in whom they obtain their highest development, happiness, and glory, both in this life and in the life to come. (*CA*, 49)

28

It is this indwelling Divine Presence of the Holy Spirit which from the day of Pentecost teaches and governs in her hierarchy, is communicated sacramentally to her members, and animates and pervades, in so far as not restricted by human defects, the whole Church. (*CA*, 130)

29

Now, when the soul sees that the external authority is animated by the same Divine Spirit, with whose interior promptings it is most anxious to comply; when it appreciates that the aim of external authority is to keep it from straying from the guidance of the indwelling Divine Spirit: then obedience to authority becomes easy, and the fulfilment of its commands the source of increased joy and greater liberty, not an irksome task or a crushing burden. (*CA*, 137)

30

Here then is the key to all the secrets of the economy of the Catholic Church concerning spiritual life. Hence the reception of the sacraments, the exercise of Church authority, and the practice of virtue are never presented as a substitute for, but as subservient to, the immediate guidance of the soul by the indwelling of the Holy Spirit. (*CA*, 219)

31
Saint Ignatius Loyola

At a later period still, in monasteries no longer cloistered, sprang up into life a new type of Christian perfection, differing in many ways from the former in its expression. The leader of this company was Ignatius Loyola, the Spanish soldier, who abandoned the sword for the more powerful weapon of the Cross. For enlarged conception, energy of execution, and boldness of design, he has not been surpassed, if ever equaled, in Church History. ("The Saint of Our Day," *Sermons*, 93–94)

August

The Holy Spirit and the World: The Renewal of the Age

As a young man, Hecker had briefly gravitated to politics as the agent of societal renewal. The mature Hecker, however, came to envision a social renewal in which individuals—who would convert to Catholicism as the answer to their deepest human aspirations—would thus be individually open to the promptings of the Holy Spirit and to the fullest appropriation of the Holy Spirit's gifts in all aspects of their lives. By combining Catholic religion and democratic political institutions, such individuals would be empowered to develop their culture and society along Catholic lines—a model for the spiritual and social renewal not just of American society but of the Old World as well.

Articles from *The Catholic World, The Church and the Age*, and *The Paulist Vocation* are the sources for most of these selections, as well as correspondence.

1

St. Alphonsus Liguori, founder of the Congregation of the Most Holy Redeemer (the Redemptorists)

Isaac Hecker is received into the Catholic Church, New York, 1844

Our soul is clothed in brightness. Its youth is restored. No clouds obscure its luster. O blessed ever blessed unfathomable divine faith. O blessed faith of Apostles Martyrs Confessors and Saints! O holy Mother of Jesus thou art my Mother. Thy tender love I feel in my heart. O holy Mother thou has beheld me! Bless me Virgin Mother of Jesus. (August 2, 1844; *Diary*, 236)

2

It is the very nature of the Catholic faith when it takes root in the heart, to make men superior to nature, and true heroes. (From a letter written during Hecker's novitiate, *PV*, 114–15)

3

What a work the Catholic Christian sees and has before him!...When I contemplate the holiness the beauty the piety the sweetness of the Catholic faith my heart is filled with ineffable joy....He cannot be a catholic who sees not in society as it is his work to do. (From a letter to Brownson, November 26, 1844; *BH*, 119)

4

Saint John Vianney, Curé of Ars

A saintly man indeed, and one gifted with a supernatural character to an extraordinary degree.... He had so much difficulty getting through his studies for the priesthood. The truth, probably, was that just at that time the supernatural action of the Holy Spirit came upon him and incapacitated him for his studies....I had something of the same difficulty myself. (*PV*, 159–60)

5

The renewal of the age depends on the renewal of religion. The renewal of religion depends upon a greater effusion of the creative and renewing power of the Holy Spirit. The greater effusion of the Holy Spirit depends on the giving of increased attention to His movements and inspirations in the soul. The radical and adequate remedy for all the evils of our age, and the source of all true progress, consist in increased attention and fidelity to the action of the Holy Spirit in the soul. (*CA*, 26)

6

The age is superficial; it needs the gift of Wisdom, which enables the soul to contemplate truth in its ultimate causes. The age is materialistic; it needs the gift of Intelligence, by the light of which the intellect penetrates into the essence of things. The age is captivated by a false and one-sided science; it needs the gift of Science, by the light of which is seen each order of truth in its true relations to other orders and in a divine unity. The age is in disorder, and is ignorant of the way to true progress; it needs the gift of Counsel, which teaches how to choose the proper means to attain an object. The age is impious; it needs the gift of Piety, which leads the soul to look up to God as the Heavenly Father, and to adore Him with feelings of filial affection and love. The age is sensual and effeminate; it needs the gift of Fortitude, which imparts to the will the strength to endure the greatest burdens, and to prosecute the greatest enterprises with ease and heroism. The age has lost and almost forgotten God; it needs the gift of Fear, to bring the soul again to God, and make it feel conscious of its responsibility and of its destiny. (*CA*, 27)

7

Men endowed with these gifts are the men for whom, if it but knew it, the age calls. Men whose minds are enlightened and whose wills are strengthened by an increased action of the Holy Spirit. Men whose souls are actuated by the gifts of the Holy Spirit. Men whose countenances are lit up with a heavenly joy, who breathe an air of inward peace, and act with a holy liberty and a resistless energy. One such soul does more to advance the kingdom of God than tens of thousands without those gifts. (*CA*, 27–28)

8

The men, the age and its needs demand depend on a greater infusion of the Holy Spirit into the soul; and the Church has been already prepared for this event. (*CA*, 28)

9

Does God ever allow His Church to suffer loss in the struggle to accomplish her divine mission? (*CA*, 28–29)

10

Let us continue our course, and follow the divine action in the Church, which is the initiator and fountain-source of the restoration of all things. (*CA*, 30)

11

What is the meaning of these many pilgrimages to holy places, to the shrines of great saints, the multiplication of novenas and new associations of prayer? Are they not evidence of increased action of the Holy Spirit in the faithful? (*CA*, 30)

12

It cannot be too often repeated to the men of this generation, so many of whom are trying to banish and forget God, that God, and God alone, is the Creator and Renewer of the world. The same God who made all things, and who became man, and began the work of regeneration, is the same who really acts in the Church now upon men and society, and who has pledged His word to continue to do so until the end of the world. (*CA*, 61)

13

There is no other way for perfection for the great mass of Christians than in the performance of the common duties of life with an eye to God. The highest noblest and most perfect life is in the fulfillment of those daily duties imposed upon us by Almighty God. This is devotion. (From a letter to Simpson, February 22, 1861; *PV*, 206)

14

I think a larger playground may be given to the action of our natural faculties and instincts without displeasing their Author. I wish to reconcile the idea of sanctity with the completeness of the natural man. Faith does not demand the depression or mutilation of our nature, or its instincts. Religion gives completeness of character. (From a letter to Simpson, February 22, 1861; *PV*, 206)

15

The Assumption of the Blessed Virgin Mary

To day is the holy day of the Assumption of the dear blessed Mary mother of our Lord and Saviour Jesus. Oh may I be found worthy of her regard and love. (August 15, 1844; *Diary*, 245)

16

The reintegration into general principles of the scattered truths contained in the religious, social, and political sects and parties of our day would reveal to all upright souls their own ideal more clearly and completely, and at the same time present to them the practical measures and force necessary to its realization. (*CA*, 161)

17

The tendency of religious minds is now to unity, as it was to disunion centuries ago; and this is a great blessing of Providence. The necessity for unity is now felt on all sides; the evils of disunion are seen in a thousand different ways. We should be untrue to Providence if we did not take our cue from this. ("The Things That Make for Unity," April 1888; *CW*, 103)

18

The question is: Can we emphasize the points of agreement, ignoring for the moment the disagreements? Yes, and safely. But it must be wisely done. As a matter of fact the very seeking for points of agreement tends to subdue the spirit of confusion, and to eliminate points of disagreement and strengthen truth. ("The Things That Make for Unity," April 1888; *CW*, 108)

19

But the reconciliation of obedient faith and intelligent liberty is the problem of the age....Let us cultivate the things that make for unity. ("The Things That Make for Unity," April 1888; *CW*, 109)

20

There is no reason why a movement towards unity should not set in, under the providence of God, in our day, just as in the sixteenth century the perversity of men brought about disunion and sects. ("The Things That Make for Unity," April 1888; *CW*, 109)

21

"The Holy Spirit fills the whole earth," acts everywhere & in all things, more directly on the minds & hearts of rational creatures, dwells substantially in the souls of the faithful, and is the light, life, soul of the Church. This all-wise, all-powerful action now guides, as He ever has & ever will, all men & events to His complete manifestation and glory. (Egypt, *PV*, 169–70)

22

The work that Divine Providence has called us to do in our own country, were its Spirit extended throughout Europe, would be the focus and element of regeneration. Our country has a providential position in our century in view of Europe, and our baptizing and efforts to catholicize and sanctify it gives it an importance in a religious aspect of a most interesting and significant character. (From a letter to Fr. Hewit, written from Rome during the First Vatican Council, 1870; *PV*, 85)

23

Father Hewit has written me about the necessity of giving our young men a thorough course of studies if we as a body are to take a leading part in the work of our day. This has been my own conviction for several years. My own mind becomes day by day more clear concerning the nature of our work and the importance of our position. As to my sight, its influence is to extend not only to our own country but to the whole world. (From a letter to his brother George V. Hecker, Rome, January 27, 1870; *PV*, 85–86)

24

The mission of the United States in the order of Divine Providence is to solve in advance the problems of Europe….If the civilization of our country is to play so important a part in the present and future of the world, our community…has a work before it in character and extent not easy to exaggerate. (From a letter to his brother George V. Hecker, Rome, January 27, 1870; *PV*, 86)

25

This movement, if we had a sufficient number of Paulists to preach, work, etc., with the spirit of our community, and could send them to England, France, Germany, and Italy, they would effect a change no one even dreams of. They would be an element of reconciliation, renewal, and regeneration. (From a letter to his brother George V. Hecker, Rome, January 27, 1870; *PV*, 86)

26

What is the fundamental idea of the Paulists? It is the idea of organizing the practical side of the Church in view of the needs of the age and the triumph of religion, for the greatest expansion of the ideal Christian life possible. What is the ideal Christian life? It is human nature in its entire force, sanctified and transformed by Christianity. (From private memoranda made in Europe during his illness, *PV*, 88)

27

This is the idea which underlies the Paulist movement, which idea needs to be practically organized in Europe in harmony with the instincts and dispositions of its different races, nationalities, and needs, in order to renew Christian life and prepare the way for the triumph of the Church. (From private memoranda made in Europe during his illness, *PV*, 88–89)

28

The Church in the United States is the offspring of the zeal, sacrifices, and blood of the Church in Europe, and shall not the child in gratitude repay the parent in the time of her trial, distress, and danger? (*PV*, 95)

29

In former days the Holy Spirit inspired souls with the vocation to go to the wilderness of America and plant the Church among the Indians. Why, in our day, should He not inspire souls with the vocation to aid the Church to recover Europe? (*PV*, 95)

30

What else has been my exile from home for, unless to prepare my soul to make my life-experience applicable to the general condition of the Church and the world in its present crisis? (From private memoranda made in Europe during his illness, 1874–75, *PV*, 90)

31

The past was for the United States, the future, for the world. To this end all particular attachments to persons, places, labors, had to be cut off, not to give a bias to the judgment, and not to interfere with my action. It was with a deeper meaning than at first sight appeared to me that I now see why I called myself "An International Catholic." (From private memoranda made in Europe during his illness, 1874–75, *PV*, 90)

September

The Church in America

One of Isaac Hecker's perennial preoccupations was the compatibility of Roman Catholicism and American values and institutions and his insistence on harmonizing the Catholic religion and American culture as much as possible. For Hecker, this was not some concession to the spirit of a secular age, but a definite evangelizing strategy. He believed that the one Holy Spirit, who inspired the questions of his own heart and the aspirations of human nature in general, also spoke authoritatively through the Church. Thus, the evangelization of American society through missionary action—aimed at the conversion of individuals and the consequent transformation of a culture—would benefit both Church and civil society. Challenging Catholics to a higher standard of moral and spiritual behavior would contribute, Hecker hoped, to improving the overall quality of Catholic life in the United States, which in turn should make the Church more attractive to non-Catholics.

In addition to previous sources, this section uses the Hecker-Brownson correspondence, the article "The Human Environments of the Catholic Faith," and the article "The Present and Future Prospects of the Catholic Faith in the United States of America."

1

Of the supernatural visitations by means of which God informed me of my mission, I have made an explicit statement to various persons, singly and in common, always under the compulsion of either obedience or necessity. The Holy Spirit gave me a distinct and unmistakable intimation that I was set apart to undertake, in some leading and conspicuous way, the conversion of this country. (From statements made toward the end of his life, *PV*, 23)

2

Oh! May Almighty God prosper our voyage, and may His sweet and blessed mother be our guide and protector on the stormy sea. And may my arrival in America be for the good of many souls who are still wandering out of the one flock and away from the one shepherd! (From a letter to his mother, London, January 17, 1851; *PV*, 25)

3

The work that seems ready for us here in the U.S. is very great, &...I trust that our labors will be a great means in the hands of D[ivine] Providence of infusing a new zeal among the faithful in this country & leading them to a more catholic & devout life which cannot help reacting on the world & making our holy religion felt as it is, & the Holy Church exercise that influence on public taste, mind & character which she must, if our country is to be one of the holy conquests of her divine faith. (From a letter to Brownson, c. April 13, 1851; *BH*, 149)

4

Often my mind is seized with the idea of a future development of our holy faith in this country. Our people are capable of great enthusiasm, & if once this is turned into the right channel, it must & will produce effects worthy of our faith & our spiritual Mother the Church. Our people *are young*, & not like europeans, & were they filled with a lively faith, new ages of faith would spring up on this continent. (From a letter to Brownson, July 29, 1851; *BH*, 155)

5

Until we have a higher tone of catholic life in our country we shall do nothing. We shall make some progress in material things, and perhaps in numbers, but in the end we shall do little for the greater glory of God, the good of Souls, or for our country. We can do no good without enthusiasm. Religious enthusiasm is the activity of the passions supernaturalized. And this is brought about by a thorough discipline—an ascetic life. If our words have lost their power, it is because there is no power in us to put into them. The Catholic faith alone is capable of giving to people a true permanent and burning enthusiasm frought with the greatest of deeds. But to enkindle this in others we must be possessed of it first ourselves. (From a letter to Brownson, September 5, 1851; *BH*, 156–57)

6

The prospects of our holy faith were never so encouraging in the United States of America as at the present moment. The most intelligent and pious Catholics regard the existing state of things as Providential and most favorable for the beginning of the conversion of the American people....The capture of a young, and already powerful, nation is a great and holy enterprise; an enterprise which the

Catholic faith alone has the grace to undertake and the zeal to accomplish. But who are called to take the initiating steps in this glorious mission? (From Father Hecker's statement to Cardinal Barnabo, Prefect of Propaganda, after expulsion from the Redemptorists; *PV*, 32–33)

7

Wednesday I said Mass in the Mamertine prison, in which St. Peter was confined by the order of Nero; and also St. Paul....There were with me four American students, and you can easily imagine that I prayed earnestly in Holy Mass to obtain for us all the zeal of the Apostles for the conversion of our country. (From a letter to Mrs. George V. Hecker, Rome, November 7, 1857; *PV*, 129)

8

My convictions grow clearer and stronger. We need as broad and unconstrained a basis to act upon as we can get, for there is no reason why we should not adapt ourselves to accept what is good in our social and political customs and institutions, as other religious orders have done here in Italy and elsewhere in Europe. My convictions gain more firmness and intensity that we are called by Divine Providence not to confine ourselves to meet but one or the other special demand of religion in our country, but to hold ourselves in readiness to meet the general wants of our people. (From a letter to the American Fathers, Rome, December 6, 1857; *PV*, 41–42)

9

In regard to a new company, it may be that Divine Providence has permitted these things to happen in order to raise up by our hands a new company,...one that would have in view the conversion of the great body of non-Catholics, well adapted to the fresh and diverse wants of a people composed of such elements as ours in America. (From a letter to the American Fathers, Rome, January 1, 1858; *PV*, 47)

10

There is no question more worthy to engage the attention of those who have at heart the spread of the Christ's kingdom upon earth, than the question whether the Catholic Church will succeed in Christianizing the American nation, as she has, in times past, the great nations of Europe. This is the great problem of the Catholic Church of this country; for the people of the United States are young, free, energetic and filled with the idea of great enterprises; a people who, of all others, if once Catholic, can give a new, noble, glorious realization to Christianity. ("The Present and Future Prospects of the Catholic Faith in the United States of North America," December 1857–January 1858; in *PV*, 265)

11

The conviction is increasing among its more enlightened citizens, that the Catholic Religion alone is able to give unity to a people occupying so vast an extent of territory, embracing such a diversified population, & of such a variety, & even conflicting interests. They feel also the need of a Religion like its own institutions which embraces the whole human race in one brotherhood, and with its divine sanction and powerful influence, will lead and assist it to realize its great destinies. ("The Present and Future Prospects of the Catholic Faith in the United States of North America," December 1857–January 1858; in *PV*, 265–66)

12

One might say that the longing after a more spiritual life is one of the principal characteristics of the American people. So far from being a nation absorbed in commerce and in accumulating material wealth, there is no other people who are so easily kindled to a religious enthusiasm, hence the success of the Methodists among them. And few will be found who are more ready to make sacrifices for the religious convictions, witness their countless churches, their Bible and Tract societies spread over that vast country. ("The Present and Future Prospects of the Catholic Faith in the United States of North America," December 1857–January 1858; in *PV*, 267)

13

What a noble conquest for the Church! What a glorious work for the exercise of the apostolic zeal of her missionaries! Never before was there a more noble and more glorious conquest offered to God's Church. In the Roman Empire, it was the battle of Catholic truth with heathenism & a nation already in decline. In the conversion of Western Europe, it was a struggle of Catholic truth with the elements of barbarism. In this new country, it is the contest of Catholic truth with an already civilized people and a young & energetic nation; one to whom Providence has certainly entrusted important destinies. ("The Present and Future Prospects of the Catholic Faith in the United States of North America," December 1857–January 1858; in *PV*, 267)

14
Exaltation of the Holy Cross

Through the cross Christ began the redemption of the world; through the cross the redemption of the world is to be continued and completed. It was mainly by the shedding of the blood of the martyrs that the Roman Empire was gained to the faith. Their conquerors were won by the toil, heroic labors, and sufferings of saintly missionaries. (*CA*, 50–51)

15

We both have double work to do. To labor to bring up the catholic body to catholic truth intellectually and morally, & to open the way to the American people to see the same truth in all its beauty....The American people will never believe, or be convinced, that we love our country, so long as we do not show genuine patriotic feeling for its interest and destiny. And they are right. (From a letter to Brownson, August 7, 1855; *BH*, 184)

16

If we wish to attract Americans we must present Catholicity to them as affirming in superabundance those qualities of character which are distinctively American—affirming them in an aspect which reveals their universality. ("The Things That Make for Unity," April 1888; *CW*, 108)

17

The American republic began afresh in the last century by the declaration of certain evident truths of reason. The law of its progression consists in tracing these truths out to their logical connection with all other truths, and finally coming to the knowledge of all truth, both in the natural and supernatural order, ending in the affirmation of universal truth and the union with the source of all truth—God. The dominant tendency of the American people is towards the law of the positive sequence of truth. (*CA*, 96)

18

Let it once be shown that the Catholic interpretation of Christianity is consonant with the dictates of human reason, in accordance with man's normal feelings, favorable to the highest conceptions of man's dignity, and that it presents to his intelligence a destiny which awakens the uttermost action and devotion of all his powers, and you have opened the door to the American people for the reception of the complete evidence of the claims of the Catholic Church, and prepared the way for the universal acceptance of her divine character. (*CA*, 97)

19

When the nature of the American republic is better understood, and the exposition of Christianity is shaped in the light of its own universal principles so as to suit the peculiarities of the American mind, the Catholic Church will not only keep her baptized American children in her fold, but will at the same time remove the prejudices existing in the minds of a large class of non-Catholics, and the dangers apprehended from the influence of republicanism will be turned into fresh evidences of the Church's divine character. (*CA*, 98–99)

20

He who does not see the hand of Divine Providence leading to the discovery of the western continent, and directing its settlement and subsequent events towards a more complete application to political society of the universal truths affirmed alike by human reason and Christianity, will fail to interpret rightly and adequately the history of the United States. It is also true that he who sees Heaven's hand in these events, and fails to see that Christ organized a body of men to guard and teach these universal truths to mankind, with the promise of His presence to the end of the world, will fail to interpret rightly and adequately the history of Christianity. (*CA*, 99)

21

But the discerning mind will not fail to see that the republic and the Catholic Church are working together under the same divine guidance, forming the various races of men and nationalities into a homogeneous people, and by their united action giving a bright promise of a broader and higher development of man than has been heretofore accomplished. (*CA*, 99)

22

The character that is formed by the institutions of our country and the Catholic character are not antagonistic. American institutions tend to develop independence—personal independence and love of liberty. Christianity rightly understood is seen to foster these qualities. For what other object did the martyrs die than to establish their personal convictions against the decrees of emperors? (*CA*, 107)

23

Sincere Catholics are among our foremost patriotic citizens, and, whatever may befall our country, they will not be found among those who would divide her into factions, or who would contract her liberties, or seek to change the popular institutions inherited from our heroic forefathers. Catholic Americans have so learned their religion as to find in it a faithful ally and a firm support of both political and civil liberty. Nowhere, on the other hand, does the Catholic Church reckon among her members more faithful, more fervent, and more devoted children than in the citizens of our republic. (*CA*, 127)

24

[The Catholic religion] is eminently well fitted to develop to the highest point the good which exists among non-Catholic Americans. Our religion is perfectly suited to the people, government, and destiny of the United States. That is one reason why it is entitled to the name "Catholic." This is a people endowed, to a greater or less extent, with natural virtues whose supernatural counterpart is Catholicity. ("The Human Environments of the Catholic Faith," July 1886; *CW*, 465)

25

Just as in the civil order the man who cannot subject his private interests to the common good is not fit to enjoy American liberty, so in the spiritual order the man who cannot obey the Church is proved unworthy of the spiritual freedom wherewith Christ has made us free. The true Catholic spirit thus enables us to understand the civic virtues of our country. ("The Human Environments of the Catholic Faith," July 1886; *CW*, 466)

26

The non-Catholic American aspires to deal with God unaided by methods or exterior helps of any kind. To come as near as possible to God by his own spiritual activity, without halting at forms of human contrivance, is his spiritual ambition. His deep religious joy is in a spiritual life which deals directly with God, his inspired word, his Holy Spirit. Now, did they but know it, these souls, by entering the Catholic Church, could secure a flight to God a thousand times more direct than they ever dreamed of. ("The Human Environments of the Catholic Faith," July 1886; *CW*, 466–67)

27

Devotions, pious practices, traditional religious methods change with times, localities, races. Here is a new place, a new time, a new race. Nothing but the changeless faith itself can be the basis of our dealing with the American people. ("The Human Environments of the Catholic Faith," July 1886; CW, 469)

28

The Catholic Church, however, cannot content itself with the mere possession of those born in the faith when there are millions of souls around her wandering into paths of error. Her mission is, as her name imports, Catholic, universal, including her apostolic zeal and embrace of her divine love, like her Divine Founder, [of] all and every soul of the human race. She cannot therefore be content without making most strenuous efforts to win those who are without her fold, especially when the prospect is so promising as in this new & vast country. ("The Present and Future Prospects of the Catholic Faith in the United States of North America," December 1857–January 1858; in PV, 268)

29

When I began to speak and labor for the conversion of the United States as a point to be aimed at, twenty-five years ago, it was thought an extravagant idea, born of a heated imagination and enthusiasm. Now it would be considered a lack of faith and zeal not to think so. (Private memoranda made in Europe during his illness; *PV*, 91).

30
Saint Jerome

The reading of the Bible is the most salutary of all reading. We say to Catholic readers, Read the Bible! Read it with prayer, that you may be enlightened by the light of the Holy Spirit to understand what you read....Read it with gratitude to God's Church, which has preserved it and placed it in your hands to be read and to be followed. (*CA*, 241)

October

Evangelization

Pope Paul VI called evangelization "the essential mission of the Church." Although Hecker did not employ that particular terminology, we can readily recognize and apply to our own situation his consistent commitment to call Catholics to the fullness of their mission to evangelize their society—and, to that end, to enhance the quality of Church life, to build up the Catholic Church in the United States. Hecker understood that *any* successful mission to non-Catholic America presupposed an effective mission and ministry within the American Catholic community. Today, we are even more apt to appreciate the importance of vibrant personal spirituality and internal Church community life for the effectiveness of the Church's mission outward to our society.

The main sources for this month of reflections

are *The Church and the Age*, *The Catholic World*, and Hecker's sermons.

1

We cannot even preserve the faith among Catholics in any better way than by advancing it among our non-Catholic brethren. Indeed, simply to preserve the faith it is necessary to extend it. It is a state of chronic disease for men to live together and not endeavor to communicate their respective good fortune. A Catholic without a mission to his non-Catholic fellow-citizens in these times, and when only a small portion of the human race has the true religion, is only half a Catholic. ("The Human Environments of the Catholic Faith," July 1886; CW, 468)

2

No virtue more becomes a Christian than zeal for souls. No virtue is more a test of every other virtue. ("The Human Environments of the Catholic Faith," July 1886; CW, 468)

3

When our lay people feel that they are unworthy of the truth unless they communicate it to their brethren outside the true fold, we shall make more progress. ("The Human Environments of the Catholic Faith," July 1886; CW, 468)

4

"Why is it that men are not happy?" We answer, that it is because either they have no religion, or are not true and faithful to it....But what we affirm is this—that until a man has solved the problems of life, Why he is here, What is his future, How he is to attain it—until he responds faithfully to them and applies all his energies to secure the end of his existence, he knows not what the truest happiness is, and has not tasted of the highest sources of joy. ("How to Be Happy," *Sermons*, 62–63)

5

Were we asked to prove the reasonableness of religion, we would point to the fact that in no subject of investigation can a man obtain so deep and lasting convictions as in that of religion. They are deeper and stronger than death, and more lasting than time. There is no object which demands the right exercise of a man's intelligence more than religion. The sources of unbelief in religion will be found, in many cases, to be the neglect of examining its evidences, or the lack of courage to believe the conclusions of one's own intelligence. ("How to Be Happy," *Sermons*, 67–68)

6

Only treat religion fairly, and you will find a reality that will enlist the entire energies and affections of your whole being. You will find what the soul always and everywhere, and in all things, seeks: you will find God. ("How to Be Happy," *Sermons*, 68)

7

Now, to make a man believe that this is the true way of arriving at his immortal destiny, nothing can be more expedient than to reveal to him that whatever truth and virtue he already possesses is but a feeble beginning of the virtues offered to his practice. You can never convert an unbeliever by striving to persuade him that he is totally depraved. ("The Human Environments of the Catholic Faith," July 1886; *CW*, 468)

8

The greater part of the intellectual errors of the age arise from a lack of knowledge of the essential relations of the light of faith with the light of reason; of the connection between the mysteries and truths of divine revelation and those discovered and attainable by human reason; of the action of divine grace and the action of the human will. (*CA*, 38)

9

The explanation of the internal life and constitution of the Church, and of the intelligible side of the mysteries of faith and the intrinsic reasons for the truths of divine revelation, giving to them their due emphasis, combined with the external notes of credibility, would complete the demonstration of Christianity. Such an exposition of Christianity, the union of the internal with the external notes of credibility, is calculated to produce a more enlightened and intense conviction of its divine truth in the faithful, to stimulate them to a more energetic personal action; and, what is more, it would open the door to many straying but not altogether lost children for their return to the fold of the Church. (*CA*, 39)

10

It is impossible, humanly speaking, that a religion can maintain itself among a people when once they are led to believe it wrongs their natural instincts, is hostile to their national development, or is unsympathetic with their genius. (*CA*, 44–45)

11

The conversion to catholicity, no matter how brought about, involves the historical argument settled in favor of the church; no man can intelligently become a Catholic without examining and deciding the historical question. But back of this is the consideration that the truths the church teaches are necessarily in harmony with my reason—nay, that they alone solve the problems of reason satisfactorily and answer fully to the wants of the heart. ("Dr. Brownson and Catholicity," November 1887; *CW*, 223–24)

12

The world is tired of what appears to many as the monotonous pounding of the historical argument and the discussion of texts. It is a sound method of argumentation, but to many it has become wearisome, and to multitudes it is not *ad rem* in the present stage of their difficulties. ("Dr. Brownson and Catholicity," November 1887; *CW*, 224)

13

I have said that by force of reason alone we could not hope to arrive at a satisfactory solution of all our difficulties. But the force of reason did this much for us: it landed us on our feet as natural men. We got human nature, however defective, in its proper and normal place. The place of man in the order of existence is in the knowledge and enjoyment of the truth. ("Dr. Brownson and Catholicity," November 1887; *CW*, 225)

14

The possibility, the practicability of the whole Catholic system is the main question with many souls outside the church. Prove that Catholic authority is conducive to the progress of human nature to a higher life, to a godlike life, and is a means to that end, and you will have no further difficulty with many non-Catholics. ("Dr. Brownson and Catholicity," November 1887; CW, 232)

15

Saint Teresa of Jesus, Doctor of the Church

Few undertakings in the Church have been conceived and carried on to success without the cooperation, in some shape, of women. The great majority of her saints are of their sex, and they are honored and placed on her altars equally with men....[St. Teresa] is represented as an authorized teacher, with a pen in hand, and with a doctor's cap. (CA, 179)

16

There is nothing, short of what is necessary to salvation, which every christian should not be willing to do, if called upon; and nothing that those whom it immediately concerns should not be willing and ready to do to render the church of Christ more attractive in the eyes of those who sincerely seek after the truth, or who are seeking for it in a more Catholic spirit, or who are anxious to find it in a more perfect form and embodiment. ("The American Congress of Churches," December 1885; CW, 415)

17

There are no souls whose error is so universal that they are utterly devoid of truth; none so vile as to be utterly without virtue. Then the truth within them must be made cooperative with the truth without which seeks entrance; then whatever virtue a bad man practises must be made use of to lead him on to the virtues which he ought to practise. Truth is kindred to truth, and virtue to virtue. ("The Human Environments of the Catholic Faith," July 1886; CW, 464)

18

To develop the mind there is never need to minimize the truth; but there is great need of knowing how to assimilate the truth to different minds. ("The Things That Make for Unity," April 1888; CW, 108)

19
The North American Martyrs

The discovery of the Western continent was eminently a religious enterprise....If the Spanish and French missionaries did not accompany the first discoverers, they followed speedily in their tracks, and the work of the conversion of the aborigines was earnestly begun. In a short time they traversed the whole northern continent from the mouth of the St. Lawrence to California, and from the Gulf of Mexico to Hudson's Bay. Sometimes missionaries were slain, but the fearless soldiers of the cross continued unceasingly their work of converting the natives and bringing them into the fold of Christ. The pages of history which narrate the self-sacrificing labors of the missionaries to the Indians are among the brightest in the annals of the Church. (*CA*, 65)

20

The true picture must be presented and contrasted with the false, so as to captivate the intelligence and enlist the enthusiasm of the active minds of the youth of the age. This is the great work that, in the economy of God, is mainly left to the initiative of individual minds among the members of His Church. It is the work of Catholic genius illuminated by the light and guided by the interior inspirations of the Holy Spirit. (*CA*, 160)

21

Let him, therefore, who would serve the Catholic Church in this generation, show her in her own true light, in her unity and universality, in all her beauty and majesty. It is this true vision of her divinity that will captivate man's intelligence, secure the unbidden homage of his will, and elicit his most heroic devotedness. (*CA*, 205)

22

If the interior and intelligible side of the Church were exposed to view in such a light that men would be led to see clearly and appreciate her essential character; if it were shown unmistakably that all her externals, when not abused or exaggerated, are strictly subservient to the securing of her essential end—union of the soul with God—there are better and stronger reasons to hope for a tide to set in towards her fold in the nineteenth century than there was to leave it in the sixteenth. For such a movement has in its favor the aim and power of the Holy Spirit, the noblest aspirations of man's soul—that for common brotherhood—and the operation of that law of unity which reigns throughout all creation. (*CA*, 205–6)

23
Isaac Hecker is ordained a priest,
London, 1849

By virtue of ordination the priest becomes a con-
ductor of God's grace to the people, *ex opere
operato*, through the means of the sacraments,
and aids them by such other rites and ceremonies
as the Church ordains. But besides this, as an individual the priest, the same as any other person in
the state of grace, is personally, through baptism
and his other graces, in communion with God,
and thereby, according to his perfection, *ex opere
operantis*, becomes a channel of grace to others.
("Personal Sanctification of the Paulist and His
Standard of Perfection," in *PV*, 122)

24

Labor to raise the standard of Catholic life here
and throughout the world, as a means of the general triumph of the Catholic faith. (August 7,
1882; *PV*, 186)

25

The greatest obstacle in the way of the success of
the conversion of the world is the divisions existing among Christians. It is these divisions and
the controversies, & hatred which they engender
that furnish among the most striking objections

to the infidel & skeptic against the truth of Christianity, & hinder the spread of Christianity. (Egypt, *PV*, 259)

26

In our intercourse with Protestants, were we to dwell more on the truths which they hold in common with us, & less on those in which they differ from us—the opposite course from that which is commonly taken—we should open the way for the more speedy return of many of them to the fold of the Church, and embrace all that she teaches. Is not this the course pointed out by Holy Scripture when it says: "Study those things which make for peace." (Egypt, *PV*, 259–60)

27

By cultivating those truths which Protestants hold in common with Catholics, they will be insensibly led to see and accept the other truths which the Church teaches, since they are logically connected with them, and rest on the same divine basis as those which they already believe. (Egypt, *PV*, 260)

28

Who knows? perhaps the time has come when men will consider impartially the causes which have brought about the deplorable religious dissensions and divisions existing among Christians, and that a movement is about to set it on all sides towards unity, and the prayer of Christ that "all who believe in Him might be made perfect in unity" will find its fulfilment. This is our hope. To contribute to this result we labor. (*CA*, 235)

29

Our power will be in presenting the same old truths in new forms, fresh new tone and air and spirit. ("Personal Sanctification of the Paulist and His Standard of Perfection," *PV*, 125)

30

Who can resist God and have peace? ("How to Be Happy," *Sermons*, 65)

31

The best sermon upon Christianity is a Christian. (May 3, 1843; *Diary*, 99)

November

Hecker's Personal and Paulist Spirituality

Hecker's outward orientation of openness to the world and his unfailing commitment to the Church's evangelizing mission remained rooted in a deeply felt, intensely lived personal experience of the indwelling presence of the Holy Spirit and the action of God's grace. From his early reflections on the spiritual life in his diary and letters, to his mature thoughts regarding the spirituality of his Paulist community, to his profoundly reflective reactions to the spiritually transforming experience of his pilgrimage to Egypt and the Holy Land, Hecker expressed what was at the heart of his own lifelong spiritual journey.

Many of the following selections are from Hecker's correspondence and from the article

"Personal Sanctification of the Paulist and His Standard of Perfection."

1
All Saints Day

Yesterday I went to the Catholic Church in west Roxbury; it was Easter Sunday. The services of the Church were to me very impressively affecting. The altar piece was Christ's rising from the tomb. This was the subject matter of the Priest's sermon. In the midst of it as he was preaching he turned and pointed to the painting with a few touching remarks turning all eyes towards it which made his remark doubly affective. How inspiring it must be to the Priest when he is preaching to see around him the Saviour the godly company of Martyrs Saints and Fathers. (April 17, 1843; *Diary*, 94)

2
All Souls Day

When, in 1843, I first read in the catechism of the Council of Trent the doctrine of the communion of saints, it went right home. It alone was to me a heavier weight on the Catholic side of the scales than the best historical argument which could be presented....The body made alive by such truths ought to be of divine life and its origin traceable to a divine establishment: it ought to be the true church. The certainty of the distinctively Catholic doctrine of the union of God and men made the institution of the church by Christ exceedingly probable. ("Dr. Brownson and Catholicity," November 1887; *CW*, 225)

3

The Church must meet & satisfy all the wants of man's heart or religious nature—and I say that the affections of the heart when pure, are no less unerring guides to truth, than the logic of the intellect. (From a letter to Brownson, September 14, 1854; *BH*, 167)

4

The Church of Christ must not only answer in general to the wants of the soul, she must also provide in a special manner for those privileged souls that her Divine Founder has called to represent His life and virtues in an eminent degree; who, unlike the young man spoken of in the Gospel, are bold with divine affection, and ready to follow the invitation of the Divine Master in humble obedience, angelic purity, and willing poverty; in a word, to copy His virtues and life of self-denial. (From a letter written during Hecker's novitiate; *PV*, 111)

5

The object of religious orders is no other than to remove all obstacles to the fulfillment of our destiny, and to furnish us with all, and the most speedy means to attain it. (From a letter written during Hecker's novitiate; *PV*, 113)

6

Happy are they who find out in their youth what all men discover at some period of life, that God, and God alone, can satisfy the inmost wants of the soul, and who consecrate themselves to His service with all the freshness and purity of their youthful energy. (From a letter written during Hecker's novitiate; *PV*, 114)

7

The backbone of a religious community is the desire of its members for personal perfection. A new religious order is the expression or evidence of an uncommon or special grace given to a certain number of souls in order to sanctify themselves by the practice of certain virtues to meet the special needs of their epoch and in this way to renew the life of the members of the Church and extend her fold. It is this or it is nothing at all; has no reason for its existence. ("Stray Thoughts," 1876–86; *PV*, 184)

8

The true Paulist is a religious entirely depending on God for his spiritual life, living in community, and labors above all to supply the most pressing needs of Church and humanity of his day. (*PV*, 185)

9

Are the Paulists Religious? Yes, and no. Yes, of their age. No, of the past; the words in neither case being taken in an exclusive meaning. The ideal is the same in all orders of religion: perfection, union with God, all that that implies. The means are substantially the same: interior fidelity to grace, prayer, detachment, mortification, all that that implies. ("Personal Sanctification of the Paulist and His Standard of Perfection," *PV*, 123–24)

10

Though we do not take vows, yet we are none the less wholly given up to the divine service. The true Paulist should be a man fitted to take the solemn vows at any moment. ("Personal Sanctification of the Paulist and His Standard of Perfection," *PV*, 124)

11

I do not think that the principal characteristic of our [Paulist] Fathers and of our life should be poverty or obedience or any other special and secondary virtue, or even a cardinal virtue, but zeal for apostolic works. Our vocation is apostolic: conversion of souls to the faith, of sinners to repentance, giving missions, defense of the Christian religion by conferences, lectures, sermons, the pen, the press, and the like works; and in the interior, to propagate among men a higher and more spiritual life. ("Personal Sanctification of the Paulist and His Standard of Perfection," *PV*, 125)

12

The virtues are, so to speak, the doors to the sanctuary of perfection. The end of perfection is the immediate guidance of the indwelling Holy Spirit. If one in our Congregation finds that poverty, or obedience, or contemplation, or liberty of spirit, or any other way, is the way that God leads him, he is free to enter by that door. Great fidelity in action, with a great and large freedom of action, should be the spirit of our Community. ("Personal Sanctification of the Paulist and His Standard of Perfection," *PV*, 126)

13

Individuality is an integral and conspicuous element in the life of the Paulist. This must be felt. One of the natural signs of the true Paulist is that he would prefer to suffer from the excesses of liberty rather than from the arbitrary actions of tyranny. ("Personal Sanctification of the Paulist and His Standard of Perfection," *PV*, 127)

14

How to cultivate strong individuality and acquire great liberty: Not by imitation of the example of others....But by looking to God alone—attention to His solicitations....Become a saint; you will have both. He who aims not at sanctity seeks not his perfection. ("Stray Thoughts," August 7, 1882; *PV*, 185)

15

It is not necessary for all to take the vows of a religious, but it is necessary for all to live holily in order to gain heaven, whoever or wherever they may be. Their souls cannot let them rest where they are. (From a letter to his family written during Hecker's novitiate; *PV*, 116)

16

Follow your *attrait* [attraction, or, what pulls one] in prayer; no one ever advanced in spiritual life *contre son attrait*. The best prayer for each one is that in which he succeeds best; from which one draws the most profit, it matter not what sort of prayer it may be called. Let us not be afraid of big names; if God gives us the grace of contemplation even in the beginning, as he does to some Souls, let us not through a false fear reject it, but correspond to his goodness by a generous confidence. If he leaves us in dryness & darkness let us endeavor to be equally willing to suffer; but never give up the exercise of meditation. (From a letter to Brownson, September 5, 1851; *BH*, 156)

17

No one who reads the Holy Scriptures can fail to be struck with the repeated injunctions to turn our eyes inward, to walk in the Divine Presence, to see and taste and listen to God in the soul. (*CA*, 24)

18

Genuine contemplation and action are inseparable. He who sees truth loves truth, and he who loves truth seeks to spread the knowledge and the practice of truth. Divine love is infinitely active, and, when it has entered the human heart and has set it on fire, it pushes man to all outward perfection and visible justice. No men have labored so zealously and so efficiently for their fellow-men, for the establishment of God's kingdom upon earth, as the saints of God. (*CA*, 162)

19

This union of the inner and outer divine action is the secret source of Catholic life; the inward principle prompts the obedience of Catholics to the divine external authority of the holy Church. From this is born the consciousness of the soul's filiation with God, whence flows that perfect love and liberty which always accompanies this divine Sonship. (*CA*, 137)

20

Revealed religion is supernatural and is full of mysteries; men can commonly best keep such a religion and realize its mysteries by the symbolism of worship. Mysteries cannot express themselves otherwise than by symbols. Intelligence which avows itself to be less than angelic is forced to have a symbolical religion if it has a supernatural one. Hence the institution of the sacraments by Christ—outward signs of inward grace, sacred symbols ordained by the Divine Founder of Christianity, by which his grace is conveyed to souls worthy to receive it. ("The Things That Make for Unity," April 1888; *CW*, 106)

21

Surely all things in the Holy Church are good; but good when we keep in view the aim of all things— the bringing of the soul nearer and nearer to God, & in more perfect union with Him. What does this for our soul, we should be faithful to; & not be led astray by taking up anything else. (From a letter to Mrs. King, 1863; *PV*, 167)

22

What you say of the Sacrament of Penance seems to me most true. It is a miracle of grace, no less for priest than for penitent. Nowhere & in no function, it seems to me, does the priest represent our Lord in His Divine character so literally as in this Holy Sacrament. It is indeed a wonder how two souls, entire strangers to each other, can at once be knit into holy bonds of friendship, so close, so sincere, so sacred. (From a letter to Mrs. King, 1863; *PV*, 168)

23

Sometimes when I speak to souls in this Holy Sacrament, I realize the words of Our Lord to be literally true: "He that heareth you, heareth Me." For it seems to me that I am only the passive, yet conscious organ of His Divine voice to their souls. (From a letter to Mrs. King, 1863; *PV*, 168)

24

The inconstant Christian should never be disheartened. Every sincere intention is meritorious. The requisite energy to gain a victory is often obtained only after the struggles of repeated defeats....The most fatal of all sins is that of discouragement. Never to despair, is in itself a great virtue, and bears with it the promise of eventual victory. ("How to Be Happy," *Sermons*, 69)

25

In reciting the Gloria and the Credo, after having been in the localities where the great mysteries which they express took place, one is impressed in a wonderful manner with their actuality. The truths of our holy faith seem to saturate one's blood, enter into one's flesh, and penetrate even to the marrow of one's bones. (Quoted in Walter Elliott, *The Life of Father Hecker*, 384)

26

We Christians might learn from them a lesson on this point and not a small one either. For prayer is the beginning of all other graces. (Quoted in David O'Brien, *Isaac Hecker: An American Catholic*, 283)

27

Whether we cooperate [with] or oppose the absolute, it is and will be all the same. He will do it. To be conscious of the Absolute always, and to cooperate with it, this is the highest action of the rational creature. This can be reached in a two-fold manner: First, by the light of reason; Second, by the additional light of Grace which are one in their source. (New York, December 17, 1875; Hecker's diary, quoted in *PV*, 218)

28

Every soul true to itself & to God has something unusual. This is not to be condemned. The natural must be guided by Divine grace, not suppressed or despised. But Divine grace must be the Master & only guide of the soul. This sure of, we can then say without hesitation—*omnis spiritus Laudet Dominum* [Let every spirit praise the Lord]: or with the Apostle *unusquisque in suo sensu abundet* [Let every man abound in his own sense; Rom 14:5]. ("Thoughts on the Spiritual Life," 1865; *PV*, 213)

29

I am willing to continue to wait on Divine Providence as things are, with constant prayer for light and strength, and continue to do as I am now doing, all I can for the Community....Also ready to resign everything with unfeigned charity and to continue to do all in my power for the good of the country. There is no other prospect before me than to be left entirely alone with no one but God. (*PV*, 189)

30

I find no step to regret, and those of importance in their bearing on my life seem to me now providential. I cannot do better than trust to that guidance which has brought me thus far, to be its agent. This is my daily, hourly, and only study; to surrender myself more completely to the guidance of God. This is my sole exercise in all that I do and suffer. God's will makes all actions equally great, all results of the same importance. Whether we live or whether we die, we are the Lord's.

Let us be united in doing His will, and in letting it be done in us! (From a letter dated August 2, 1864; *PV*, 82)

December

A Future for the Church Brighter Than Any Past

We conclude our year-long journey with Servant of God Isaac Thomas Hecker with a final series of reflections—the majority from Hecker's later years—which witness to his continued confidence in the providential action of the Holy Spirit in the Church and his abiding hope for "A Future for the Church Brighter Than Any Past"—words inscribed on his monumental tomb in the church of the parish he founded to be the vibrant center from which his Paulist community would go on to disseminate the story of his life, continue his mission on behalf of the Church, and promote his hopeful spirituality throughout contemporary North American society.

These final reflections are from *The Church and the Age, The Paulist Vocation,* and correspondence.

1

Through these clouds which now obscure the Church the light of divine hope ought to pierce, enabling us to perceive a better and a brighter future, for this is what is in store for the Church and the world. That love which embraces at once the greatest glory of God and the highest happiness of man should outweigh all fear of misinterpretations, and urge one to make God's hand clear to those who are willing to see, and point out to them the way to that happier and fairer future. (*CA,* 9)

2

The meditation of the great truths of Christian faith is the source from which the inspiration must come, if society is to be regenerated and the human race directed to its true destination. He who looks to any other quarter for a radical and adequate remedy, and for true guidance, is doomed to failure and disappointment. (*CA,* 22)

3

The notes of the divine institution of the Church, and the credibility of divine revelation, with her constitution and organization, having been in the main completed on the external side, the notes which now require special attention and study are those respecting her divine character, which lie on the internal side. (*CA*, 36)

4

The trials and sufferings of the faithful are the first steps toward a better state of things. They detach from earthly things and purify the human side of the Church. From them will proceed light, and strength, and victory. (*CA*, 30–31)

5

But how many souls in secret suffer sorely seeing the Church in such tribulations, and pray for her deliverance with a fervor almost amounting to agony! Are not all these but so many preparatory steps to a Pentecostal effusion of the Holy Spirit on the Church, an effusion, if not equal in intensity to that of apostolic days, at least greater than it in universality? (*CA*, 31)

6

The Church…has already entered on this path of presenting more intimately and clearly her inward and divine side to the world, for her deepest and most active thinkers are actually engaged, more or less consciously, in this providential work. (*CA*, 49)

7

God is not extinct nor are religious motives effete. The mistake...consists in supposing that the present is the finality of Christianity, whereas the hand of God is opening the way by purifying His Church, by directing the movements of nations and the issues of the world, to the end that she may shape the coming future beyond all past experience in her progressive approach to the perfect realization of her Divine Ideal. (*CA*, 158–59)

8

*Immaculate Conception of the
Blessed Virgin Mary,*

Patronal Solemnity of the United States

This morning I said mass in St. Peter's. Our affairs are in the hands of God. I hope no one will feel discouraged, nor fear for me. All that is needed to bring the interests of God to a successful issue is grace, grace, grace, and this is obtained by prayer, and if the American Fathers will only pray, and get others to pray, and not let anyone have the slightest reason to bring a word against them in our present crisis, God will be with us, and Our Lady will take good care of us. (From a letter to his brother George V. Hecker, Rome, September 2, 1857; *PV*, 31)

9

Daily my confidence increases that Providence has destined me to do an important work for our country. Let us strive to be more faithful to his grace & inspirations, and he will grant us the petitions of our hearts. (From a letter to Brownson, April 7, 1855; *BH*, 179)

10

What will not this young nation accomplish for religion, when the energies which are now spent in her steamships, railroads & vast commercial enterprises are enkindled by the Catholic faith into a religious enthusiasm! ("The Present and Future Prospects of the Catholic Faith in the United States," December 1857–January 1858; *PV*, 268)

11

Here in Geneva I have met several distinguished persons, both Protestant and Catholic, and the light and profit which they have derived, according to their own acknowledgement, from the views which I have expressed, ought to be to me the source of great consolation and support. It appears to me that Divine Providence is employing me in a larger field and a more important one than my past, and that by and by this will become more and more clear. However this may be, all is in His hands. He will do as He will. (From a letter to friends in America, 1874; *PV*, 87)

12
Our Lady of Guadalupe,
Patronal Feast of North and South America

The Catholic faith is the only persistently progressive religious element, compared with the increase of population, in the United States. A striking proof that the Catholic Church flourishes wherever there is honest freedom and wherever human nature has its full share of liberty! (*CA*, 57)

13

The age, we are told, calls for men worthy of that name....Men, assuredly, whose intelligence and wills are divinely illuminated and fortified. This is precisely what is produced by the gifts of the Holy Spirit; they enlarge all the faculties of the soul at once. (*CA*, 26–27)

14

The increased action of the Holy Spirit, with a more vigorous co-operation on the part of the faithful, which is in process of realization, will elevate the human personality to an intensity of force and grandeur productive of a new era to the Church and to society—an era difficult for the imagination to grasp, and still more difficult to describe in words, unless we have recourse to the prophetic language of the inspired Scriptures. (*CA*, 39–40)

15

Christianity once more will be perfect in one, and, uniting its forces for the conversion of the world, will direct humanity as one man to its divine destination. (*CA*, 161)

16

O sincere seeker after truth! Did you but know it, the path lies open before you to a perennial fountain of truth, where you can slake to the full that thirst which has so long tormented your soul. O sincere lover of your fellow-men! There is a living body which you may enter and co-operate with, whose divine action is realizing a heavenly vision for the whole human race, brighter and more beautiful than the ideal which so often haunts your lonely dreams! (*CA*, 167–68)

17

The phase of Catholicity which is now coming slowly to the light will gather up all the rich treasures of the past, march in response to every honest demand of the interests of the actual present, and guide the genuine aspirations of the race in the sure way to the more perfect future of its hopes. (*CA*, 168)

18
Isaac Hecker is born, New York, 1819

It is my 25th birthday; here let me offer myself to Thee for Thy service oh Lord. Is it not what I should? Am I not thine? Thou didst create me and ever hast sustained me. Thine I am. Accept me oh my God as thine, a child who needst most thy love and protection. (December 18, 1844; *Diary*, 272)

19

To me my life has been one continued growth; and hence I have never had any desire to return to any part or period of it. This applies as well to my life before I was received into the Church as after. My best life was always in the present. (From a letter dated New York, August 2, 1864; *PV*, 82)

20

All our difficulties are favors from God; we see them on the wrong side, and speak as the block of marble would while being chiseled by the sculptor. When God purifies the soul, it cries out just like little children do when their faces are washed. (On the guidance of the Holy Spirit, *PV*, 133)

21

The soul's attention must be withdrawn from external, created things, and turned inward towards God exclusively before its union with Him; and this transformation is a great, painful, and wonderful work, and so much the more difficult and painful as the soul's attention has been attracted and attached to transitory things. (On the guidance of the Holy Spirit, *PV*, 133)

22
Isaac Hecker dies, New York, 1888

There was once a priest who had been very active for God, until at last God gave him a knowledge of the Divine Majesty. After seeing the majesty of God that priest felt very strange and was much humbled, and knew how little a thing he was in comparison with God. (Quoted in *The Life of Father Hecker*, 380)

23

The soul is created for God, its happiness consists in the possession of God, and, reason as we will, it is no one's fault but our own if we fail in obtaining God. And this is the aim of religion: to solve the dark problem of life and place man in the possession of God. ("How to Be Happy," *Sermons*, 67)

24
Christmas Eve

We would not deny the Absolute under any form of its manifestation; we should hold ourselves culpable if we did, but let it be understood that while we would not do this no more than to deny our blessed Lord and divine Saviour we do hold that the Catholic Church is the divine appointed medium by which Man is given a new birth and saved from Sin...reunited to God [and] made partaker of the glory and blessedness of the Angels of Love and Light and an inhabitant of Heaven and brother of Jesus. Jesus is the incarnation of the Absolute God; all prior manifestation of God was qualitative and relative. (July 18, 1844; *Diary*, 222)

25
Christmas Day

Christ has come. Christ is here, now upon earth. Christ ever abides with men, according to His word. What the age promises men is the rending asunder the clouds of error which hinder them from seeing that Christ is here. What the age promises and men most need is the light to enable their eyes to see that the Incarnation involves Christ's indwelling presence in His Church acting upon man and society through her agency until the consummation of the world. (*CA*, 256)

26

The Church will present herself to their minds as the practical means of establishing the complete reign of the Holy Spirit in the soul, and consequently of bringing the kingdom of heaven upon earth. This is the ideal conception of Christianity, entertained by all sincere believers in Christ among non-Catholics in Europe and the United States. This exposition, and an increased action of the Holy Spirit in the Church co-operating therewith, would complete their conviction of the divine character of the Church. (*CA*, 50)

27

May not the fullness of time have come, seeing that the Church has been, as an external organization, greatly strengthened by the definition of the [First] Vatican Council, and seeing the great facility of communication throughout the world by electricity & steam, when by a greater effusion of the Holy Spirit in the life of the Church, the great work of the conversion of the world will be brought about? (Egypt, *PV*, 249–50)

28

To bring back into the fold of the Church a people who once were in it, & have strayed from it, is a more difficult task than to convert a people who are ignorant of Christianity. (Egypt, *PV*, 249)

29

The Holy Spirit is at work among Chinese, Moslems, and all nations, peoples and tribes, in every rational soul. The love of God, so to speak, compels this. We may not see or understand its secret operations, but the truth of this is none the less true for that. We may be nearer to the conversion of these races, & the unity of the race, & the triumph of Christianity, than any one of us is aware of. (Egypt, *PV*, 169)

30

Those portions of the church which are in an apathetic and torpid state we may hope will be roused up; a multitude of sluggish and unfaithful Catholics become reanimated with the spirit of faith; and the unity, sanctity, catholicity, and apostolicity of the church—the immortality of her life, the divine authority of her teaching, the irresistible and universal power of that spirit which is in her—be manifested with a brightness which

will make forever glorious the close of the nineteenth century, whose opening was so very dark
and inauspicious. ("The Approaching Council of
the Vatican," June 1869; *CW*, 366)

31

How does Father Hecker? In body? Not so well
for several months, but now improving. In spirit?
Living and working in the dawning light of an
approaching, brighter, more glorious future for
God's Holy Church. A future whose sun will first
rise on this continent and spread its light over the
world. (From a letter to a friend; *PV*, 99)

Bibliography

Catholic World. New York/Mahwah, NJ: April 1865—. Issues from 1865 to 1901 are archived online by the digital library Making of America Journals at http://quod.lib.umich.edu/m/moajrnl/browse.journals/cath.html.

Elliott, Walter. *The Life of Father Hecker*. New York: Columbus Press, 1898.

Farina, John, ed. *Isaac T. Hecker: The Diary: Romantic Religion in Ante-Bellum America*. Mahwah, NJ: Paulist Press, 1988.

Gower, Joseph F., and Richard M. Leliaert, eds. *The Brownson-Hecker Correspondence*. Notre Dame, IN: University of Notre Dame Press, 1979.

Hecker, Isaac T. *Sermons Preached at the Church of St. Paul the Apostle, New York, During the Year 1863*. New York: D. & J. Sadlier, 1864.

Hecker, Isaac T. *The Church and the Age: An Exposition of the Catholic Church in View of the Needs and Aspirations of the Current Age*. New York: *The Catholic World*, 1887.

O'Brien, David J. *Isaac Hecker: An American Catholic*. Mahwah. NJ: Paulist Press, 1992.

Paulist Prayer Book. Mahwah, NJ: Paulist Press, nd.

The Paulist Vocation. Mahwah, NJ: Paulist Press, 2000.